PORTRAIT OF HERTFORDSHIRE

By the same author

PORTRAIT OF LEICESTERSHIRE

Portrait of HERTFORDSHIRE

by

BRIAN J. BAILEY

ROBERT HALE · LONDON

First published in Great Britain 1978

ISBN 0 7091 6603 6

Robert Hale Limited
Clerkenwell House
Clerkenwell Green
London EC1R 0HT

PHOTOSET AND BOUND BY WEATHERBY WOOLNOUGH,
WELLINGBOROUGH, NORTHANTS,
AND PRINTED IN GREAT BRITAIN BY
LOWE & BRYDONE LTD., THETFORD,
NORFOLK

CONTENTS

ILLUSTRATIONS

Between pages 48 and 49

Between pages 96 and 97

MAP

PICTURE CREDITS

The copyright photographs listed above were supplied as follows:

The author, 2, 4, 7, 10, 20, 22, 23, 27, 32; Janet and Colin Bord, 1; Tony Craddock, 9 (by courtesy of Tony Stone Associates Ltd), 24, 25, 30, 33; EMI Elstree Studios, 12; Hawker Siddeley Aviation Ltd, 13; N. McMillan, 11; Kenneth Scowen, 8, 14, 15, 17, 18, 31, 34; W. Stephenson, 35; Peter Thompson, 3, 6, 16, 19, 21, 26, 29; Victoria and Albert Museum, 28; Tony Ward, 5

ACKNOWLEDGEMENTS

All the main published works on which I have relied are listed at the end of the book, but I have received much valuable help from various public and private sources, to all of whom I should like to express my gratitude.

I am most grateful to all the sources of photographs listed, for helping me to accumulate a wide-ranging pictorial portrait of Hertfordshire, and I must mention in particular my friends Tony Craddock, Nevil McMillan, Kenneth Scowen and Peter Thompson.

I am enormously indebted to my old friend Van Phillips, whose erudition and fine judgement have saved me from errors in both content and style.

Marilyn Prejac's typing from my text, some of which was in scribbles I was scarcely able to read myself, was of almost uncanny accuracy.

I suppose in a way it is absurd for an author to print acknowledgement of his wife's help. It should go without saying that it is the partnership which has produced the book. Nevertheless, since it is not the convention to include the author's wife on the title page, I here express the customary thanks I owe to my wife, twelve months of whose life would have been so much easier if I had been otherwise occupied. Among other things, she has spent many long hours driving me round the county to preserve me from the hazardous necessity of having to do two things at once: be thoroughly observant whilst keeping my eyes on the road.

To

J. B. PRIESTLEY,

the Old Master

of English prose portraits

INTRODUCTION

A HUNDRED AND FIFTY YEARS AGO, Hertfordshire presented a very different face to the portraitist from the one we see now. Almost totally agricultural, such industries as it possessed were themselves by-products of agriculture. But no county in England has changed more dramatically, and it now presents strong contrasts. Sometimes likened in its shape to a kettle, it would be more accurately described as a pressure cooker.

Yet one could be forgiven for thinking that, except in St Albans perhaps, nothing much has ever happened there. In spite of the large number of 'substantial residences' (as the estate agents call them), and the wealthy landowners who have made Hertfordshire their home, it is not noted for its architecture, though St Albans Cathedral and Hatfield House are famous exceptions. Nor has it any cultural history to speak of, though it has been home to writers as diverse as Bulwer-Lytton, Bernard Shaw and Graham Greene.

Its peculiar fascination lies in the survival of much of its old character and its appealing, and occasionally beautiful, landscape, with narrow country lanes leading between fields of ripening corn to villages whose greens, cottages and churches look as if they have grown up together out of the soil.

Much of Hertfordshire's charm is under threat, however, and I have allowed the newly dominating influence of its major roads to dictate the shape of this book. They fan out through the county like the rays of the sun - life-giving at the proper distance but fatal too close. Roads were traditionally called 'ways' in Hertfordshire, and I have taken the hint for my chapter headings.

A recent boundary change posed the problem of how to deal with Barnet, which became part of Greater London in

1965, in exchange for Potters Bar and district. Was it a fair swop? Unquestionably so, in my view, and I have been somewhat relieved to bypass Barnet. Any author writing on Greater London is welcome to it.

If the face in this portrait might once have been thought of as plain, but with a twinkle in the eye, it is now ravaged, not by age (for Hertfordshire is quite a young lady), but through becoming the unwilling mistress of the metropolis, which, to prevent her from leaving the bed, grasps her tightly by the throat.

I

THE NATURE OF HERTFORDSHIRE

"HELL," as Shelley wisely conjectured, "is a city much like London", and Hertfordshire is perched uneasily over the inferno like a potato, somehow contriving to remain uncooked, though badly scorched underneath. With little more than four hundred thousand acres, the county is one of England's smallest, but its population is greater than that of many larger areas. It is, for instance, 'home county' to more people than Lincolnshire, although the latter has an area four times Hertfordshire's size.

Paradoxically, the preservation of its rural character seems, to some extent, to be due to the very feature which appears to threaten it most. The major trunk roads which shoot up through Hertfordshire like great flames from the London furnace, overheating the towns they pass through, like Watford, St Albans and Hatfield, seem to serve at the same time as safety valves, like the steam vents in a pressure cooker, saving the villages that lie between them from being done to a frazzle.

Hertfordshire – particularly its southern half – is prime commuter territory, and the roads and railways which bring traffic into London from the Midlands and the north also carry commuters in their thousands, travelling into the city to do their day's work and then out again, weary escapees from the metropolis to subtopia. In trains from Euston, St Pancras, King's Cross and Liverpool Street; by 'tube' from Paddington and Baker Street; in motor cars and Green Line buses on the M1 and A1(M), A41, A5, A6, A10 and A11, they come pouring out to their homes in what they are pleased to regard as 'the country', although they usually bring their city news and their city standards with them, and the residential villages are so totally different from the real country villages that it is only the concrete jungle of the capital that could delude them into believing they live in 'rural' surroundings.

Three new towns have been created in Hertfordshire since the Second World War to absorb some of the explosive London population, and in the 'fifties the population of Hertfordshire increased faster than that of any other county in Britain. And it is not only people that increase. The number of private cars in the county has been consistently above the national average for many years, and the number of heavy goods vehicles on the county's roads increased by a phenomenal 2,800 per cent between 1957 and 1973, compared with a national increase of 900 per cent. And the London takeover continues with plans for new motorways – the North Orbital Road and the M11 – and the Lea Valley Regional Park: a huge playground for north London. So the pressure builds up all the time, and it is an interesting, if depressing, question how long it will be before the lid blows off.

We can squeeze precious little comfort from the fact that Hertfordshire's proximity to London has always constituted a threat to its nature, without actually destroying it. The county has not had to suffer such a massive invasion since Julius Caesar led his troops across the Thames. The character of Hertfordshire has been changed more in the last hundred years than in the thousand years preceding them. But although some of its towns are new, most of its great roads are not. The Icknield Way, which crosses the county in the north, was a prehistoric track along the ridge of the Chilterns. The A5 still follows – more or less – the course of the original Roman road later called Watling Street, whilst the ancient Ermine Street was the origin of our A10, and Akeman Street roughly our A41.

So the rural character of Hertfordshire has survived two thousand years of growth and development along its major routes, and agriculture has remained its chief preoccupation despite the introduction of all sorts of manufacturing industry, not least among which has been aircraft construction. Thus the county presents strong contrasts, and although the influence of London is never far away, I would not subscribe to Sir Nikolaus Pevsner's statement that "one's eyes are hardly ever allowed to forget" its closeness to the metropolis. It depends whether your eyes are trained on civilization or on nature. I sometimes find it hard to believe that nowhere in Hertfordshire can you get forty miles away from Piccadilly Circus.

Hardly more than a couple of miles off the frantic A41, in the south-west of the county where London's long reach seems most likely to throw a knock-out uppercut, I know a wood where the wild cherry grows. Spectacular in spring with a rich blue carpet of bluebells, the wood is abundant in late summer with blackberries and the sloes of the blackthorn, and austere in winter when blackbirds and thrushes rustle about in the blanket of dead leaves, and grey squirrels scamper along the branches of oak and beech. At dawn the peace is broken only by the distant bark of a village dog or the calls of birds startled by human intrusion, but in the night you might hear the eerie call of a fox or the cry of an owl. From the damp ground near the stump of a fallen tree the erect stinkhorn, *Phallus impudicus,* grows; and a rabbit hole, well hidden in the undergrowth, has been enlarged for use by the fox that ate its original inhabitant.

One can emerge from the shade of trees into a little glade where, on a hot summer's day, the air is alive with the hum of flying insects, the rustle of grasshoppers, the songs of willow warblers and lesser whitethroats and the raucous cries of jays and woodpigeons. Ringlet, orange tip and fritillary butterflies flutter and settle in the brambles. The heat of the sun shimmers as it beats down between the surrounding trees, on clover and buttercups and rosebay willowherb, wild roses and the blossom of the elder trees. The cares of civilization, represented only by the distant sound of church bells on a Sunday, evaporate the moment I enter this wood, and this is the other, older side of Hertfordshire, which has not changed so much from the land beloved of Charles Lamb and Izaak Walton. It was a county renowned for its market towns and village greens, healthy air, fine estates, quiet country lanes, and the clear, gentle streams in which watercress could be cultivated. And though the estates and the lanes, as well as the air and the water, are somewhat polluted now, there is still plenty of the old Hertfordshire left for those who care to seek it. It is a county rich in common land, and in spite of its small size, it has more village greens than any other county in England.

It is hardly surprising that Oscar Wilde set part of *The Importance of Being Earnest* in an imaginary Hertfordshire village where the formidable Lady Bracknell wonders if the air has anything to do with the inclination of the younger people in the play to get engaged. But Wilde's view of the train service to London was a trifle optimistic. Ten minutes after Lady Bracknell has told her daughter it is time to go, she insists that they have "already missed five, if not six, trains". And this in the middle of the afternoon!

This land we call Hertfordshire rose out of the sea, like Venus, white and virginal, when the tides receded from the north-west of the area in the Pliocene Age - rather recent in geological terms - and a huge saucer-shaped layer of chalk was formed, through the deepest part of which the River Thames now flows. The rims of the saucer are the Chiltern Hills at its northern edge, and at its southern, the North Downs of Surrey and Kent. Glacial thaws carved a deep gap through the Chilterns near Tring but left the valley dry, and this is known as a 'wind-gap'. The chalk base of Hertfordshire is 600 feet thick, and later earth movements tilted it down towards the Thames Valley, so that Hertfordshire's rivers and canals, like its roads, have a roughly north-south direction, although its chief river the Lea, rising in Bedfordshire, flows across country near Harpenden to Ware before turning south to join the Thames near the East India Docks. Some experts maintain that, before the Ice Ages altered the landscape, the River Thames flowed through the sites of Rickmansworth and Hertford. Underneath the chalk there is an older layer of impervious clay, which forms an underground reservoir by holding the water that soaks through the chalk, and provides many natural springs from which prehistoric wanderers drank when men first set foot in the district.

In the north of the county, there is a layer of hard sandy chalk called Totternhoe Stone, which was quarried for building material at one time, though chiefly in Bedfordshire, and in the upper layers of chalk throughout the county a good deal of flint was deposited, which has also been used extensively for building. This was the 'shingle' left behind by the falling sea level. The Opies reported in their *Lore and Language of Schoolchildren* a local belief in Watford that it is lucky to find a stone with a hole in it. Such a find is not uncommon where flint lies thick on the ground, and the belief is a survival from several in Hertfordshire about the special properties of flint, one of which was that if a holed flint was hung in a stable, it would prevent a horse from sweating.

In the southern parts of the county, towards the dip of the Thames basin, layers of clay, gravel and alluvium were deposited during the Ice Ages, and there has been quarrying on a small scale in these areas too. The London clay runs across the county roughly south of a line from near Rickmansworth to Hertford and Ware, and then swerves north-east to the Furneaux Pelham area. Hertfordshire's mineral deposits are of no great significance, however, and its chief building material since Elizabethan times has been brick.

The earliest human penetrations of the county were along the river valleys and via the Icknield Way. Celtic nomads of the Iron Age left a few signs of their presence about the ancient trackway that follows the Chiltern ridge and forms a link between the Berkshire Downs and East Anglia and the sea. The track first enters Hertfordshire across the Tring peninsula and then, after passing near the source of the Lea at Leagrave, re-enters the county as the A505 near Hexton, crosses the River Oughton at Ickleford and then, passing through Letchworth and Baldock, becomes the county boundary for a short distance before leaving Hertfordshire just beyond Royston.

Most of the earliest signs of man in Hertfordshire have been discovered in the vicinity of this prehistoric road, and the clearest remaining Iron Age hillfort is the so-called

Ravensburgh Castle, half a mile south-west of Hexton village on a spur of the Barton Hills. It is oval in shape and 22 acres in extent, with a 50-foot ditch and banks 18 feet high to protect it. It seems likely that this fort was a settlement for Celtic people for a time, though the thick forest which covered most of Hertfordshire made it inhospitable, and the heavy clay soil discouraged agriculture by the primitive ploughs these people possessed. Other Iron Age earthworks exist at Arbury Banks at Ashwell, near the source of the River Cam, and at Wilbury Hill near Letchworth, also beside Icknield Way. There are also isolated barrows along the course of the road, notably on Royston Heath.

The first people to settle in Hertfordshire on any large scale, however, and to make the land serve their interests, were the Belgic tribe whom the Romans called the Catuvellauni. They invaded the area during the first century BC, via the river valleys, and drove out such earlier settlers as they found. Equipped with heavy ploughs, they set up their camps, cleared parts of the forest and cultivated the soil. It was these people, who made love in their wattle and daub huts and war in their chariots to defend themselves against the Romans, whose blood flowed in the veins of the first known Hertfordshire natives. The tribal capital of the Catuvellauni seems to have been established at Wheathampstead, the area of which is still flanked by two ditches, both over a thousand feet in length. One is known as the Devil's Dyke and the other as the Slad. It was Sir Mortimer Wheeler who excavated this site in the early 'thirties and discovered its importance in pre-Roman Britain.

By the time of Julius Caesar's second expedition to Britain in 54 BC, the Catuvellauni occupied a large area north of the Thames, stretching from Oxfordshire to Essex and northwards into Northamptonshire. When Caesar's army prepared to cross the Thames, it found the native forces lined up on the far bank behind a line of pointed stakes, more of which were concealed below the water-line. And Caesar had already seen the effectiveness of the British chariots. "They begin," he wrote,

> by driving all over the field, hurling javelins; and the terror inspired by the horses and the noise of the wheels is usually enough to throw the enemy ranks into disorder. Then they work their way between their own cavalry units, where the warriors jump down and fight on foot. . . . Their skill, which is derived from ceaseless training and practice, may be judged by the fact that they can control their horses at full gallop on the steepest incline, check and turn them in a moment, run along the pole, stand on the yoke, and get back again into the chariot as quick as lightning.

Nevertheless, a combined attack by Caesar's experienced and well-organized cavalry and infantry forced the natives back, and the Romans marched on the stronghold of the tribal chief, Cassivelaunus, which was "strategically placed among woods and marshland", according to Caesar, with large numbers of men and cattle there.

Whether this stronghold was, in fact, the tribal capital at Wheathampstead is, to say the least, uncertain. No evidence of Roman activity has come to light there, and the *Victoria County History* assumes the site of Verulamium to have been the battleground – on equally slender evidence. It is not proven that the battle occurred on Hertfordshire soil at all. But wherever this stronghold *was* situated, Caesar's troops attacked it from two sides and overpowered the natives. Cassivelaunus then came to terms with the invaders and disappears from history, and from that point onwards the story of ancient Hertfordshire becomes concentrated around Verulamium, the city built by the Romans on the River Ver, where St Albans now stands, and to which we will return.

After the sudden departure of the Roman legions from Britain in the fifth century, the forests were left once again to encroach on the land cleared for agriculture, until the Saxons came, driving the Celtic tribes west and beginning to clear the land more thoroughly and to cultivate the soil with their heavier ploughs, creating villages as the nuclei of their open-field system of farming, which was to last for many centuries. Hertfordshire was then part of the Kingdom of

Mercia, and most of the county's villages date from this period.

When the Viking invaders began their raids in the ninth century, the Hertfordshire area was held by the Saxons, and the River Lea formed part of the frontier of the subsequent Danelaw. Mercia, already split up by tribal warfare in which Alfred had extended his Kingdom of Wessex, was further ravaged by the Scandinavian pirates, who later invaded Wessex and drove the Saxon defenders into the south-west, only to be driven back themselves by Alfred. Hertfordshire then became part of Wessex, and many a savage battle must have taken place on its soil as the Danes raided villages across the border, but this land remained under the control of Alfred, and the kings of Wessex duly became the kings of England, until the Norman Conquest. The fortresses built by Alfred's son, Edward the Elder, during his victorious campaign against the Danes, included two at Hertford, and as they were the headquarters of the territory in which they stood, it was thus that the county of Hertfordshire came into being.

The last time the villages of Hertfordshire suffered destructive raids was at the hands of William of Normandy, during his strategy of forcing England to surrender without invading London, and it was at 'Beorcham' that he was offered the English throne. It is uncertain whether this was Berkhamsted, once called Great Berkhamsted, or Little Berkhamsted, the village near Hertford. It is reckoned that Hertfordshire then had a population of about eighteen thousand, mostly engaged in agriculture, though there was still a great deal of thick forest at that time.

The population was reduced dramatically in the fourteenth century by the Black Death, and some of the county's villages were totally lost, either as a direct result of the plague, or through migration to more hospitable sites, or because landowners destroyed villages to create pasture for sheep when agricultural labour, scarce after the plague, cost them double in wages. In 1349 the Abbot of St Albans and forty-seven of his monks died, and in the following year, some desperate villager scratched a Latin inscription on a wall in Ashwell church: "Wretched, wild, distracted, the dregs of the people alone survive to witness."

People began to move from the country into the towns, beginning a process that continues to the present day, and which was accelerated by the growth of industry and the coming of the railways. To take two examples at random – between 1801 and 1901 the populations of Braughing and Little Gaddesden were considerably reduced, whilst those of Ware and Berkhamsted were trebled in the same period. It would be a mistake to suppose that the great influx of 'foreigners' into Hertfordshire was entirely due to the growth of industry and commuterism, however. The need for extra labour at the harvests had brought itinerant workers from Ireland and elsewhere who eventually settled in the corn-growing country. And the agricultural depression towards the end of the nineteenth century brought many Scotsmen here – dairy-farmers who took advantage of cheap land rents to convert the heavy soil to pasture land, which required less labour. Grazing cattle can be seen especially on the eastern side of the county bordering on Essex. Sir Henry Rider Haggard, best known as the author of *King Solomon's Mines* and *She,* was a rural economist who noted at the turn of the century that there were more Scotsmen than natives on some Hertfordshire estates, and that good land near a railway line, which facilitated the marketing of dairy produce, was rented at much higher rates than land a few miles from the nearest station.

The native blood of Hertfordshire consists of Celtic, Roman, Saxon and Norman, with perhaps a little Danish, but here we must take note of a curious circumstance. For the typical native of Hertfordshire, instead of being tall and blond as we should expect of a county so strongly influenced by Nordic settlers, is, on the contrary, short and dark, like the Welshman. Indeed, it was said at one time that the heads of Hertfordshire and Essex men were considerably smaller than those of other Englishmen. It would seem that a pocket of the Celtic inhabitants, whose type and culture were driven west by successive invasions, remained in the Hertfordshire area, although no obvious traces of them, except this physical character, are to be found in the people today, and names of Celtic origin are extremely rare in the county. So the native population of Hertfordshire is just a little mysterious. Perhaps the natives intermarried with the Romans on a larger scale here than elsewhere - brought into closer sympathy with the occupying forces by the devastation visited on them by the warlike tribes to the east. Nowadays, of course, with the huge influx of people from London and elsewhere in this century, there is probably very little native blood left in the southern half of the county, but it is worth noticing that the incidence of blood group O, which is said to be characteristic of people of Celtic descent, is considerably higher in the Berkhamsted area than in Hemel Hempstead, where a large proportion of the population is imported. Similarly, Hitchin has a higher percentage of O group blood than the new towns of Letchworth and Stevenage.

It seems clear that the influence of London has helped to prevent Hertfordshire from developing a unique personality of its own. Its cultural aspirations are inhibited by London, just as its needs are supplied by the capital. It makes little distinctive contribution to the nation's theatre, music, sport, architecture or gastronomy, because London overwhelms it, although it has made some significant contributions to literature. Hertford's County Hall may be its administrative centre, but in no other sense does the county appear to have a 'capital' at all. When you escape from the apparent dictatorship of the metropolis, the different parts of the county seem to lack a sense of unity, so that it is much easier to believe, for example, that Tring is in Buckinghamshire, Royston in Cambridgeshire and Bishop's Stortford in Essex, than that the three have any connection with one another. Except for the remnants of its dialect, and its flint churches with their 'Hertfordshire spikes' (token spires), there is not very much that is peculiar to the county in its 'civilized' aspects except what the twentieth century has brought it, and that not always welcome.

The county's landscape, however - away from the ever-present road works – is one which has not changed in its essential features for many centuries. Enclosed fields with their hedges and trees have replaced the open fields with their strip farming, but basically Hertfordshire is a county of arable land on which the traditional crops are wheat and barley. Corn was exported from the county as long ago as the thirteenth century, when ships sailed up the River Lea to be loaded at Hertford.

Hertfordshire's agriculture has been a triumphant battle against its poor stony soil, begun by the Saxons and continued ever since. High fertility has been gained by the aid of rich manure brought from London, and improved drainage by the device of digging up chalk and spreading it over the fields, so that in due course Hertfordshire became known as the chief corn-growing county of England. The west specialized in wheat, and the north and east in barley, whilst the southern strip on the London clay produced hay. And from its rich harvests grew two of its earliest industries – from wheat the straw-plaiting trade and from barley the making of malt for the breweries. And I should add here that Hertfordshire has always been noted for the vast number of inns and ale-houses where the natives consume the product they help to make.

The county's wild cherry trees are descendants of the once-numerous cherry orchards which produced a sweet fleshy fruit known as 'Hertfordshire Black'. The word 'Cherry' occurs frequently in the names of farms, houses, streets and fields in the south-west – Cherry Cottage and Cherry Tree Farm are to be found everywhere. The beech, with its shallow spreading roots adapting readily to the thin soil, has colonized the wooded chalk slopes of the Chilterns in the west, while elsewhere the hornbeam is to be found more frequently in Hertfordshire and Essex than anywhere else in England.

Evolution is changing the landscape even as I write, for Hertfordshire has been a badly hit victim of Dutch Elm Disease. Although the trouble, caused by elm bark beetles, has been known in this country since the early part of the century, it is only since the epidemic which began in 1968 that devastation on a large scale has been caused, and the Forestry

Commission has admitted that the disease is out of control. Many a place called 'The Elms' or 'Elm Tree Farm' will soon be without any visible means of support for its name. Over a third of the county's three hundred thousand elm trees were reported as dead or dying in 1975, and although this is a lower proportion of loss than in some other counties (due to the fact that Hertfordshire has a large number of the slightly less susceptible smooth-leaved elms), the disfigurement of the countryside in summer is still a dismaying sight. Trees scheduled for felling can be seen everywhere as I write, marked with chalk crosses like the doors of medieval houses stricken by the plague. There is only slight consolation in the thought that these stately English trees were largely planted in the hedgerows when the Enclosure Acts came into force, and with arable farmers now requiring larger fields in which to operate machinery economically, many elms and hedges would probably have disappeared anyway in the coming decades.

Agriculture and village life are the keys to the real nature of Hertfordshire folk. The large towns are untrustworthy guides with their great influxes of alien population, bringing alien accents and attitudes with them. That southern England 'snootiness' which northerners so abhor is to be found in the towns, not in the country. Furthermore, so far from being snobbish, the natives were at one time known as 'Hertfordshire Thickheads'. "If a man fall," it was said, "he'll come to no harm as long as he falls on his head." More soberly, the *Victoria County History* asserts that: "Educationally, Hertfordshire has not in ancient times or in modern times been prolific of great results." That view probably cannot be maintained of the larger towns in this century, but country folk move more slowly, for all the equality of opportunity the county offers today. It may seem to some deplorable that young persons at small country nurseries, or smallholdings which sell their own produce not far from the capital city of England, have difficulty in adding up a column of figures when a few items are purchased. But their lives are concerned with milking cows, feeding chickens, getting in the harvest and mucking out stables – subjects not found in the average school curriculum! What do they want with mathematics and the arts of working in city offices? Their kingdoms are not of that world.

Nevertheless, it is hard to avoid the conclusion that there is a certain inbred docility in the natives of Hertfordshire, perhaps originating in the relatively unhindered domination of their land by the Romans and successive invaders up to and including the vast commuter population of the present day. Although the Peasants' Revolt had one of its main sources in Hertfordshire, and despite the fact that the county was on the side of Parliament in the Civil War, one has the impression that the people have generally been resigned to their fate at the hands of those who have ruled them. Religious dissent was slow to take hold in Hertfordshire, and the county's early support for the Trade Union movement was singularly half-hearted. Attempts have been made to explain the latter circumstance on the lines that the widespread straw-plaiting work of women and girls put the family economy on a level sufficient to ensure the workers' contentment, but I am not impressed by this argument. Wages were low in Hertfordshire, and children had to be put to work at straw-plaiting when they were very young in order to earn their keep. Straw-plaiting was a symptom of docility, not a cause.

Before the introduction of farming machinery, the schools closed when the harvest was in progress so that every available hand – man, woman and child – could be in the fields, and itinerant harvesters would be employed to help out too, assembled ready for work at five o'clock in the morning. The harvest was the most important event of the year. The livelihood of the people depended on it, and everything else automatically took second place to it. If the sun ripened the corn early one year, the schools closed early; if rain delayed the harvest the next year, the school holidays were extended. And when the corn had been gathered, the gleaners went over the fields, picking up the corn which had been left by the harvesters. This was a day-long job for women and girls.

The harvest is still one of the rural distinctions of Hertfordshire. You can see corn being harvested almost anywhere in Britain, but not on such a huge scale. Fields of wheat and barley, green in June, when the wind sends great ripples galloping across them like herds of wild horses, turn to rich buff and gold by the end of July, and men and machines get to work to reap the rewards of their ploughing and sowing earlier in the year. Picture no. 5 shows threshing being done on a farm at Walkern by a method which preceded the advent of the combine-harvester. The corn is being fed into a threshing drum which separates the grain without breaking up the straw, as happens in the modern machinery. The straw can thus be used for thatching roofs. The introduction of combine-harvesters resulted in a serious reduction of the amount of wheat-straw available for such crafts.

When the reaping was done by hand, a great deal of folklore and superstition surrounded the harvest, which began with the traditional drink called 'wetting the sickle' and ended with the plaiting of straw into corn-dollies, those ritual survivals of a harvest thanksgiving far more ancient than the festivals in the Christian churches, which perforce embraced a 'pagan' propitiation ceremony to the goddess of fertility.

Workers in the straw-plait trade were once a cause of much concern to the Christian moralists and preachers. Illiteracy was one thing, but worse than their "lamentable ignorance" was the fact, as one village rector put it, that "a large average of the women have illegitimate children, and some at such an early age as quite to startle even those who are at home in criminal statistics".

Criminal statistics, indeed! Well, Hertfordshire was a county ruled by the rich landowners. Agricultural wages here were lower than in the north of England, and you had to take what amusement you could find, unsophisticated though it might be. The native humour has a tendency towards irony. The smallest field in the parish is liable to be called Thousand Acres, and one at Kimpton is called World's End, although good humour did not extend to the naming of unfertile fields of bad soil, which were bluntly called Hungry Hill, Starve Acre or Lousydell. A villager explaining a shrub in his garden to a local journalist once said: "That be rosemary, sir. They do say it only grows where the missis is maaster, and it do grow 'ere loike woild foire." The pun is in favour here, too – "a pistol let off at the ear", as Lamb wrote, "not a feather to tickle the intellect".

The survival of ancient traditions marks the difference between the real Hertfordshire people and the sophisticated foreigners. The rural villages have grown out of the land; the commuter towns have been superimposed on it. Centuries of agriculture have implanted the experience of the land in the hearts and minds of the true natives. The fertility of the soil and the changing seasons have shaped their folklore. This is a land of ghosts and witches and evil spirits, of pagan superstition and benighted story-telling, in which it is a bad omen to see a hare, and the heritage of their country sport is to be seen in the large number of public houses still called The Cock or The Fighting Cocks. Pub names in Hertfordshire are predominantly a 'Cock' and 'Bull' story, with Plough, Barleysheaf and Waggon and Horses among other agricultural favourites. I have seen people stopping their cars near my house before Christmas to cut branches from the holly trees – something that would never have been done by country people years ago, since it was supposed to bring ill fortune, the holly being a sacred tree.

Singularly little has been written about the Hertfordshire dialect, probably because the movements of population have been excessive here and the true dialect has been obscured as a result. But characteristic speech can still be heard in the north of the county, where it merges into Midland, and in the east, where it is influenced by Cockney. Its chief feature is the long 'a'. Elderly natives call the county 'Haarf'r'sheer'. "Me ole spooert" is a characteristic term of endearment, the word 'old' being much used in a rhythmic rather than literal sense: "It's a queer ole day, ent it?" or "It's a fraasty ole mornin', maaster." But then: "Oi ent gawt toime ter stan' 'ere a-chattin', oi gart a jarb o' work ter git on wi'." If you talk too much, you are "all jaw, loike a sheep's 'ead".

Farmworkers might enjoy "y'aarb tea" whilst seeing to

their odmedods, bogarts, maulkins or shewalls, these being customary names for scarecrows, all having their own distinctive features. The labourers would take the tea out to the fields with them when going to work, "aafter brestfust", and it would keep them going until it was time to "goo 'oom". There is an inclination to say 'done' instead of 'did' - "Oi done it laast week", and children nowadays tend to sound the 'g' at the end of a word as if it were 'k' - "somethink else" - an obvious result of Cockney infiltration.

The 'aarb tea' was made from agrimony, camomile or yarrow, generally by pouring boiling water on a quantity of the flowers and leaves, and straining it when brewed. Yarrow tea used to be highly thought of as a remedy for rheumatism, and this may be a rare Celtic survival, for the plant's Latin name, *Achillea,* derives from the fact that Achilles, according to Homer, cured the wounds of his soldiers with it.

One of the few native gastronomic inventions is boiled gooseberry pudding, made by mixing green gooseberries with dough and boiling like plum pudding. It is then eaten with butter and sugar. The first Sunday in July, when the fruit is ready for picking, was traditionally known as Gooseberry Pudding Sunday. Another natural dish in Hertfordshire was watercress soup, made by adding finely chopped watercress to the liquid from boiled potatoes and leeks, and stirring in some cream.

The social distinctions in the county are most marked along a south-west to north-east axis. One end is dominated by posh residential villages and new towns, and the other is relatively unspoiled agricultural territory. The south of the county has long been a Conservative stronghold, but the Tory hold is less secure in the north. In the nineteenth century, a duke, a marquis, five earls and a miscellaneous assortment of lords and knights had their seats here. They were collectively celebrated in 1894 in an extraordinary book, *Hertfordshire Leaders*, into which the author poured more adulation and split infinitives than I have ever seen between two covers. One pictures the personages in its pages casually deciding the fate of Hertfordshire over after-dinner port at Brooks's or the

Athenaeum. "I longed to read," a friend of mine remarked, "that one of them had been caught in bed with the cook." But if one of them had, this particular writer would not have told us so. If they were "upright churchmen" and "staunch Conservatives", they qualified for a place in this sycophantic volume, which goes so far as to call Hertfordshire the "Mecca and El Dorado of Conservatism". But although all its subjects, it would seem, had "sterling qualities", the author was not, in all cases, able to enlighten us as to what these qualities were. He set them up on pedestals to be admired for their packaging rather than their content, like the merchandise in supermarkets. We shall summon the ghosts of a few of these lost leaders to appear before us in the ensuing pages; relics of "a world of pomp and state buried in dust". I ought to add here, though, that the county's proximity to London has obviously meant that a large number of public figures - statesmen and actors, writers and high-class prostitutes - have lived in the county though not natives of it. I shall make it clear when a *native* of Hertfordshire is being discussed.

It is hardly surprising that the rat-race is the favourite modern sport in the south of the county. Ambitious executives establish their status in the pecking order with their choice of homes and motor cars in an area of soaring property prices. Those who can't get high mortgages are jealous of those who do. Deviousness creeps into business and social relationships, with everyone jostling for position in an extravaganza of one-upmanship. To live in Harpenden is better than to live in St Albans, but to live in Radlett is better still. Hertfordshire is, of course, a victim, not a cause, of this delusion.

Delusions of one sort or another afflict a great many of the people who suffer the stresses of London life, and for those who choose cerebral abdication as their method of escape, Hertfordshire provides sanctuary in its liberal sprinkling of mental hospitals. At the 1971 census, by far the largest group of people not included in private houses were the patients in the county's psychiatric hospitals - nearly ten thousand, half of whom were in the institutions scattered round St Albans.

The county's chief historians are unreadable now except by

the devoted antiquary. They compiled vast catalogues of manorial histories, family pedigrees and memorial inscriptions, which tell us everything there is to know about the ruling classes and the contents of churches, but nothing about what Hertfordshire was like, its nature and people being outside their dry, academic interests.

The first was Sir Henry Chauncy, who published his work in 1700, and whatever else may be said of his history, his was the immense research on which the books of his followers were largely based. Chauncy was born at Yardley Bury, now Ardeley, in 1632, called to the bar in 1656, and made first Recorder of Hertford, being knighted by Charles I in 1681. His history is pedantic in style and littered with inaccuracies, but he claimed to have been diverted from his original design by concern over the "ruinous machinations of a degenerate member of his family", who blued the family fortune.

Chauncy's book was followed in 1728 by that of Nathaniel Salmon, who updated the earlier work. Salmon was curate of Westmill until he resigned the living on finding himself unable to acknowledge Queen Anne as his sovereign. He then took up medicine at Bishop's Stortford before going to London to devote himself to literature, thus saddling us with a multitude of words which would have dissolved mercifully into thin air if only he had remained in the pulpit.

Next in the field was Robert Clutterbuck, born and bred in Watford. Of his text, his name says everything, but the three huge volumes of his work are distinguished by their beautiful engravings, which make them by far the best illustrated of any book on Hertfordshire, before or since. Mere photographs blush for want of beauty beside the splendour of these old plates.

Then came John Edwin Cussans, a bearded and bright-eyed Victorian born in Plymouth, who published learned works on heraldry and spent fifteen years on his massive three-volume history of Hertfordshire. Was it worth it? Well, Cussans was a very able writer who came to life when writing from the heart (he accused Chauncy of being "singularly unsusceptible of ecclesiastical beauties"). But he felt it necessary to follow the pattern set by his predecessors, and his 'history' is ruined by its confounded thoroughness, carefully reprinting the unvarying epitaphs of every Tom, Dick and Harry who "departed this life" or "fell asleep" leaving enough money to buy a headstone in the local churchyard.

We may pick up a few tips here and there from these rigorous detailers, but I should like to wander through the towns and villages and fields of Hertfordshire with a broader view of the county in mind, hopefully presenting a more lifelike portrait of the subject than is possible by minute examination of all the spots on its face. Those readers who distrust impressionism will have to turn back to what we might call the 'School of Chauncy'.

II

WAY OUT WEST

THE A41 bursts into Hertfordshire near Bushey, keeps close to the M1 past Watford, and then parts company with the motorway to thunder through Hunton Bridge, Kings Langley, Berkhamsted and Tring before making off for Aylesbury and Birngham, having twanged the nerve-strings of everybody *en route*. To make the strings supposedly less taut, motorway loops are to bypass Hunton Bridge and Kings Langley; Tring having already been so bypassed. First the roads ruin the towns and villages as the volume of traffic increases, and then the new roads built to relieve them ruin the countryside as well.

That place which Charles Lamb, a century and a half ago, was able to call the "pretty village of Watford", has been described more recently by another poet, John Betjeman, as "Hertfordshire's largest, ugliest and noisiest town", and you can't say fairer than that. We shall do well to get Watford behind us at the outset, for nowhere in the county is the irresistible spread of the monster London more evident and more threatening. Bushey, Oxhey, Watford, Croxley Green, Aldenham, Hunton Bridge and Abbots Langley have already fused together like lumps of molten plastic in the heat of the inferno and, as a well-known resident of Hertfordshire might say, you can't see the join.

Let Midlanders beware. The Green Belt is growing tighter round London's expanding waistline, and it will have to be slackened by a few notches soon. Unless there is some unforeseen long-term reversal of the population growth, London's bit of country will, in a few decades, start around Newport Pagnell, and the dread city of Milton Keynes will become the north-west frontier that Harrow-on-the-Hill once was.

The origin of Watford itself is obscure. The name is not mentioned in Domesday Book, but the village was probably included in the manor of Cashio. Watford stands on a hill between the Rivers Gade and Colne, and is supposed to take its name from 'Wata's ford', Wata being, of course, one of those hypothetical Saxon landowners we dream up to account for something we cannot otherwise explain. If Wata did not exist, it was necessary to invent him.

Watford belonged to St Albans Abbey until the dissolution, when it became the property of the Crown, and at the same time Cashio was acquired by Sir Richard Morrison for 170 pounds. The village had been granted a weekly market by Henry I, and it grew up at a modest rate along its High Street until the first half of the nineteenth century. Daniel Defoe was able to call it "a genteel markate town . . . very long, having but one street". In 1801 Watford's population was three and a half thousand. Its thirteenth-century church was set back a little from the main street and the houses lining the Market Place had long gardens, many with pigsties. It had one or two breweries and three silk mills, and a barn at the back of a public house in which travelling players gave performances, and where the young Henry Irving once appeared. This was the beginning of a theatrical tradition which has survived to the present day, though somewhat precariously, and despite its nearness to the West End. The Palace Theatre in Clarendon Road is the only old living theatre in the county, and its proscenium stage creaks beneath performances by both amateur and professional companies. Built in 1908 as a music hall, the theatre has been graced by the presence of Marie Lloyd and many other well-known players, and now operates on subsidies from the local council and the Arts Council, maintaining a respectable attendance rate by keeping its seat prices below those of the London theatres.

In the nineteenth century, London began to affect Watford in ways which were to change it for ever. First the Grand Junction Canal came close to the little town, to be followed in 1837 by the Euston–Boxmoor section of the London and Birmingham Railway. A wider variety of manufacturing began, and in the later part of the century the growth of a commuter population was already well under way. Watford was a village no more, but a bustling industrial town with engineering works and a powerful position in the printing and associated industries. In 1894 it became an Urban District, and by 1901 its population had rocketed to nearly thirty thousand, and that figure was nearly doubled in the next thirty years. It built itself a big Town Hall in 1940. London retailers opened new branches there, and London Transport took underground lines out to it. It has the county's only team in the Football League.

Now Watford is a characterless place, a mere appendage of London, and one is glad to get out of it. Indeed many a motorist is very *relieved* to get out of it, since its one-way traffic system can create the illusion in a stranger that he is trapped in a labyrinth which has no exit.

Printing, paper-making, process engraving and printing-ink manufacture have been predominant in modern Watford, and one of the town's buildings which would have seemed least likely a century ago is the distinctive brick factory of Odhams Press, designed by Sir Owen Williams, who was later such a leading light in the launching of Britain's motorway system, which had its beginning right here. The M1 originally started near Watford and ended at Crick in Northamptonshire – a sort of umbilical cord with no mother at one end and no child at the other.

Watford's parish church of St Mary, solidly built of flint, stands off the High Street in the town centre's only remaining refuge from Bedlam. Members of the Morrison and Essex families, who owned Cassiobury on the west side of the town, lie buried here. Sir Richard Morrison's great-grand-daughter married Sir Arthur Capel of Little Hadham, and their son, also Arthur, was created Earl of Essex in 1661. It was he who built the original mansion of Cassiobury, a fine house with superb woodcarving by Grinling Gibbons which was incorporated in the rebuilding carried out by the fifth Earl, George, at the beginning of the nineteenth century. His wife, the actress Kitty Stephens, described

Cassiobury as ". . . a very pretty house and more full of comforts, curiosities and pretty things than any house I ever saw".

Our Victorian author, C. A. Manning Press, unwittingly damned his contemporary Earl of Essex with faint praise by enlarging on the Earl's ancestors at the expense of the Earl himself, but he could not bring himself to tell us that the first Earl committed suicide in the Tower following his involvement in the Rye House Plot, to which we shall come later.

The Earls of Essex lived at Cassiobury for over 250 years, but in 1927 the house was demolished and the park bought by the council, so that Watford's people can now enjoy the open air and the trees by the River Gade and perhaps - if they happen to be there on 13 July - meet the ghost of the first Earl, who was said to visit Cassiobury each year on the anniversary of his death.*

Further upriver towards Hunton Bridge is another estate, The Grove, where Sir Robert Taylor built a red-brick mansion in 1756 for the Earl of Clarendon, one of whose descendants, a hunting, shooting and - for all I know - fishing Lord Lieutenant of the county, said that "were it not for the sports of the field effeminacy and deterioration would ensue, and there might be some truth in the accusation which sometimes even now is hurled against us, that we are only a nation of shopkeepers".

I do not know any shopkeepers who would subscribe to the notion that effeminacy and deterioration are necessary qualifications in the retail trade, and after all, it was a shopkeeper of sorts who built the most magnificent house in this part of Hertfordshire - Moor Park near Rickmansworth. It is now, almost unbelievably, a club house for the well-known course where golfers drive off across Capability Brown's bunkered landscape, but The Grove, even worse, belongs to British Rail, and is used as a training centre.

Moor Park belonged to St Albans Abbey until, late in the fifteenth century, it passed to George Neville, the Archbishop of York and Lord Chancellor, who built a house there called

* I should mention here that 'Bury' is a word to be encountered frequently in this book. The country houses that in other counties are called 'Hall' or 'Place' are usually called 'Bury' in Hertfordshire.

The Moor. After his conviction for high treason the property passed to the Crown, and was granted by Henry VIII to Cardinal Wolsey, who lived there for a time before Hampton Court took him to Middlesex. In 1655 Moor Park entertained Sir William Temple and his wife for their honeymoon. Temple was the cultured and accomplished diplomat who was largely responsible for the Triple Alliance, and he adored his brilliant wife, Dorothy Osborne, famous as the writer of some of the most delightful love letters in English literature. Temple was so impressed by Moor Park that he called his own house, where he employed Swift, by the same name.

Soon afterwards Moor Park became the property of the Duke of Monmouth, the Merry Monarch's son by Lucy Walter. But this new owner was soon to be dragged trembling from a ditch and executed for treason on Tower Hill, where Jack Ketch swung his axe so many times without killing the Duke that his name was used to signify the opprobrium in which every succeeding executioner was properly held by the public. They finally had to sever the Duke's head with a knife.

Monmouth's widow, having remarried, sold Moor Park in 1720 to Benjamin Styles, a merchant who had made a fortune from the South Sea Bubble, and it was he who built the present house, spending £130,000 on rebuilding Monmouth's mansion and commissioning Sir James Thornhill and Giacomo Leoni for the design and decoration. It is in classical style, fronted by a magnificent portico with four Corinthian columns, and the interior is lavishly painted by Italian artists with themes from Greek mythology. Styles had a hill removed on the north side of the house, to give himself a fine view of the Chess valley, and Alexander Pope satirized this in his *Moral Essays*, implying that Styles had let the north wind into his house merely for the sake of overlooking a dead plain.

Later owners of Moor Park included Lord Anson, the pirate and circumnavigator of the world, who died here; the Marquis of Westminster; and Lord Leverhulme. The Rickmansworth U.D.C. bought the estate in 1937, and has built houses on part of the park, but the restored mansion, which is open to the public on Monday afternoons, is the most opulent nineteenth hole any golfer ever dreamed of.

Rickmansworth itself, though perilously close to both London and the Watford conglomeration, takes its name from the rich water meadows around it (Ryke-mereswearth), though unfortunately it retains little of its old character now. It is the headquarters of the Three Rivers District, from the fact that the Gade, the Chess and the Colne meet there (not to mention the Grand Union Canal), and it is regarded as a high-class residential area. It was here, to Basing House, 44 High Street, that William Penn brought his charming wife, Gulielma Springett, to live for four years. Penn, the much-persecuted disciple of George Fox, was the founder of Pennsylvania and its capital Philadelphia, which he peopled with his Quaker converts who had suffered in the nation's prisons whilst he, the son of a famous admiral, had enjoyed the society of rather better-off friends, the comforts of court, and the confidence of the King.

On the west side of the town towards Chorleywood is a public house called Land of Liberty which is so named, ironically enough, not in honour of William Penn, who *did* set up a land of liberty of sorts, but of Fergus O'Connor, who *failed* to do so. O'Connor was the Chartist Member of Parliament who established a Cooperative Land Society at Rickmansworth in 1846, but it was declared illegal some years later and sold. And if further irony in the lives of these brief residents of Rickmansworth were needed, it is surely that both the successful man and the failed one suffered from mental illness towards the ends of their lives. Penn married Gulielma at King's Farm, Chorleywood, in 1672, and both Chorleywood and Rickmansworth have little streets named after him. Fox visited the Penns at Rickmansworth, and the Society of Friends made many converts in Hertfordshire.

Chorleywood was once called Charley Wood, and according to a story which Cussans was "almost ashamed to accord . . . the dignity of print", it was so named because one of the royal Charlies – the Merry Monarch or his old man – once rested in the wood there! However that may be, it is one of the county's most select residential areas, spilling over the border into Buckinghamshire, and on the Hertfordshire side surrounding one of those large commons of which the county has an inordinate number. Chorleywood's is rich in gorse and overlooks the lovely Chess valley, although this is now traversed by a section of the controversial M25 Outer Orbital Road, an ugly scar across the landscape which is helping to make Watford into a massive road junction for north London traffic.

Among the sometime residents of Chorleywood have been Sir Henry Wood, the only true begetter of the annual promenade concerts named after him, and Sir George Alexander, who is buried in the churchyard by the common. Sir Henry, who was responsible for introducing a great deal of foreign music to English audiences for the first time, died at Hitchin in 1944, but he lived here at Apple Tree Farm. Sir George Alexander was among the last of the great actor-managers, and after a time under Irving at the Lyceum, fame came to him at the St James's Theatre, which he took over and ran for the twenty-six years before his death.

Alexander was not a flamboyant or imaginative actor, but a serious, handsome and dignified man who ran his theatre with great distinction and performed his parts with what William Archer called "his unfailing tact, elegance and self-restraint". His best and his worst moments came when he staged Oscar Wilde's *The Importance of Being Earnest*, for it was Alexander who had encouraged Wilde to write it, and it was a brilliant success at once. But George Alexander was a child of his time, and joined the general hypocrisy of Victorian England after Wilde's conviction for homosexual practices, by removing the author's name from the posters and programmes at the theatre, whilst continuing to make money from the production. He also snubbed Wilde in the street after his release from prison, but later made some amends for his shameful action by making Wilde a regular payment for the plays he had acquired very cheaply through the author's bankruptcy.

To the south of Chorleywood, the county pushes out an amoeba-like limb to its most southerly point, occupied by the village of West Hyde, hemmed in on one side by lakes and the Colne, and on the other by the busy road to Slough and Uxbridge. To the north, a group of villages enclosed by the county boundary and the A41 includes Sarratt, Chipperfield, Bovingdon and Flaunden.

Sarratt is distinguished by its long village green and by the Norman church of Holy Cross, unique in the county because of its saddleback roof. But the church and the green are a considerable distance apart. When Chauncy published his history of the county in 1700, he said that the church was – as one would expect – in the centre of the village, but it is not so now. The centre has shifted to the green, which is surrounded by houses in the oddest assortment of architectural styles you could hope to find.

According to Chauncy, Sarratt derives its name from Syret, "a Saxon, who, I suppose, was an ancient Possessor of it". But Syret is probably as mythical as Wata, because Sarratt was, in fact, a Roman site. There is Roman brick in the church, as well as flint and Hertfordshire 'puddingstone' (a conglomerate of flint pebbles and silica, common in the area), and in a wood near the hamlet of Belsize there is a rectangular earthwork which was probably the defensive ditch of a Belgic homestead in early Roman times. Close to the church is a large house called Goldingtons, a nineteenth-century manor house owned by the Clutterbuck family, to whom the county historian was related. But in Rosehall Wood there is supposed to be the site of the older manor house of Rooshall. Though this has disappeared without trace, it took its name from a lord of the manor named de Roos, and there is some vague ghost story associated with it. Rosehall Farm and Green remain as witnesses to its one-time reality, and the farm, at the highest point in the parish, has a Tudor rose set in the plaster of its kitchen ceiling.

For some obscure reason, the local nickname for this village was "backward Sarratt", but it was evidently quite forward in some respects, for in 1485 Thomas Hemingforth was ejected from his living here for 'apostasy', which probably meant that he was a disciple of Wycliffe; and a hundred years later one

John Butler had to make a public apology for the "somewhat irregular proceedings" by which he indicated his Puritanism.

There was an unfortunate family named Baldwin here in the early eighteenth century who were much troubled by what, in those days, was regarded as "possession by devils". John and Rebecca Baldwin had four daughters, and the three youngest, Anne, Rebecca and Mary, fell victims to a form of temporary insanity in which they suffered fits and delusions, and Mary, the youngest, had periods of dumbness and blindness. The eldest girl, Elizabeth, remained unaffected, and their father held frequent prayer meetings to which were attributed their eventual recovery, Mary having imagined that her evil spirits departed from her when she vomited a large piece of flesh which crawled away snivelling and crying. The fact that all three girls were between twelve and sixteen at the time is sufficient indication for our wiser age that the onset of puberty had more to do with their mental disturbances than evil spirits, but occurring at a time when the witch-craze was hardly over in England, it is not surprising that these events at Sarratt caused such a stir that they are still recalled in the history books.

Flaunden presents us with something of a mystery, too. The present village is well over a mile away from the church which used to serve it. Flaunden is listed as a deserted medieval village, but it is far from clear when and why it was deserted. It used to be in the parish of Latimer, in Buckinghamshire, and the site of the old church is tucked into a corner of Hertfordshire, in a little spinney beside the Chess. All that can be seen of it now are a few carved stones lying near a spring which feeds a small stream, but in this century it was possible to find the "picturesque ruins" of the Greek-cross shaped church with traces of thirteenth-century wall paintings and the tomb of Richard Prince, an eighteenth-century lord of the manor.

At one time three or four tiny cottages were built against the walls of the church (there is an engraving of it in Clutterbuck) and Cussans relates a nice story that a woman from one of these was showing some people round the church when one of them remarked that he would like to attend service in it. "Well," the woman said, "tomorrow is the regular day, but I do hope and trust it will rain, and then the parson won't come, for I've got one of my best hens a-sitting on thirteen eggs in the pulpit, and she won't come off till Tuesday." There is little sign of anything more than a few cottages ever having been in the meadow near the old church, and it seems odd that the village should have been re-established so far away from the old site, which appears pleasant and hospitable. Flaunden's new church was the first building designed by Sir George Gilbert Scott, in 1838, and the font and one of the bells were taken from the old church, the other two original bells having been lost.

North of Flaunden, where Venus Hill lies incongruously adjacent to Hogspit Bottom, is Bovingdon, which also has a Victorian church, rebuilt on the site of the old. They used to post a man on the tower so that he could nip down and ring the bell when he saw the parson from Hemel Hempstead coming along the road, but if the weather was bad, the parson would not come, and Cussans tells us that many a corpse was left in the church for four or five days before a clergyman could be found to perform the burial service. Perhaps the village's isolation accounts to some extent for the influence of Lollardry there. Two villagers were executed in the fifteenth century for their involvement in the Oldcastle Rebellion. There was a stronghold of Lollardry in the Chilterns in Buckinghamshire, centred round Amersham, but it did not penetrate very far into Hertfordshire. Bovingdon's disused R.A.F. airfield is the scene of some local controversy, having been proposed as a site for a prison. As the airfield is mainly in Buckinghamshire, however, we will not dwell on the dispute here.

Chipperfield is well known for its common, where village cricket is played on the delightful green shaded by lime trees and overlooked by church, manor house and the old Two Brewers Inn where, it is said, prize-fighters were once trained. The manor house is a fine building of the seventeenth century with a later front of red brick and splendid wrought-iron gates on to the common. Legend has it that Richard III once rode across the common when staying at Langley Palace, and was jeered at by the village women, so in revenge the king decreed that henceforth widows of the parish should not be allowed their dowries from their husbands' estates, as had been the custom when men died intestate.

The horse is an animal in special favour throughout this south-western corner of Hertfordshire. Riding-schools and livery stables seem to surround every village, and equestrianism seems to have replaced elocution as the fashionable requirement for a well-brought-up girl. The horse is three times more popular with girls than with boys, and psychologists and others derive amusement from the fact that the peak of horse popularity coincides with puberty. Whether or not these troops of awkward-looking mounted girls travelling the country lanes are unconsciously getting satisfaction from what Dr Desmond Morris gleefully calls "a long series of rhythmic movements with the legs apart" is, to my mind, a matter of little consequence. For most it is a passing phase, but a few blossom into comely horsewomen who present an image of style and breeding never to be seen behind the wheel of a car (which might *also* be seen as a sexual substitute).

Kings Langley and Abbots Langley were once a pair of rural villages given their distinguished names by the presence of a royal palace in the one case and ownership by the Abbot of St Albans in the other. Langley means long meadow. Both have interesting stories to tell, but neither presents the attractive face now that it once did. Abbots Langley is practically in the grip of Watford, with a large mental hospital and an aerodrome at its doorstep. The hospital used to be the 'Metropolitan Asylum for Imbeciles'.

Kings Langley shifted its centre of population centuries ago to take advantage of the trade offered by Akeman Street, only to find itself today sitting astride the extremely unpleasant A41. Fortunately for its future, perhaps, it is to be bypassed by a motorway loop, which might help to preserve its tottering reputation as a 'posh' residential village. It has found it very hard to sustain that image in recent years. The raised pavement along one side of its main street has a wooden rail to which the women shoppers tether their poodles. It is only when you peep at the backs of its commonplace shop fronts that you realize the street has some very interesting old buildings, mostly of red brick. Its oldest inns were in business early in the seventeenth century.

It was much farther back in history when Kings Langley earned its name, however, for here, as Nathaniel Salmon so flatly put it, "the rubbish of royalty exists". Of the two kings most closely associated with Kings Langley, and both murdered, one is celebrated by Marlowe and the other by Shakespeare. The village was known as Chiltern Langley until the late thirteenth century, when a local carpenter was employed to make traps for the wolves that still roamed the Chiltern Hills at that time. Edward I's wife Eleanor acquired the manor and enlarged or rebuilt the house there, and grossly spoiled her young son the Prince of Wales, who in due time became the homosexual King Edward II. Piers Gaveston spent much time at Langley with the King, and when he was executed by the barons for his evil influence on the sovereign, Edward had him buried in the Dominican priory close to the palace.

The other king of the poets was himself buried in the same priory church after his death at Pontefract, though his body was later removed by order of Henry V and laid in Westminster Abbey. Richard II was the son of Edward the Black Prince and nephew of John of Gaunt and Edmund, Duke of York, who was born at Langley Palace. Richard succeeded to the throne when he was but ten years old, in 1377, and inherited a kingdom ravaged by the Black Death, at war with France, and warming up for the Peasants' Revolt. It was a position that even a powerful and mature ruler would not envy, and Richard was quite unequal to it. He tried to strengthen his authority, but was more effective in introducing the handkerchief to English society, and at length his cousin Henry Bolingbroke seized the throne and had Richard murdered.

Shakespeare set a scene of his play in the Duke of York's garden at Langley, where the gardener (gifted with uncommon eloquence) expounds for the benefit of his servants on the state of the realm through the analogy of the garden plants.

Gardener: Go, bind thou up yon dangling apricocks,
Which, like unruly children, make their sire,
Stoop with oppression of their prodigal weight:
Give some supportance to the bending twigs.
Go thou, and like an executioner,
Cut off the heads of too fast growing sprays,
That look too lofty in our commonwealth:
All must be even in our government.
You thus employ'd, I will go root away
The noisome weeds, which without profit suck
The soil's fertility from wholesome flowers.

Servant: Why should we in the compass of a pale
Keep law and form and due proportion,
Showing, as in a model, our firm estate,
When our sea-walled garden, the whole land,
Is full of weeds, her fairest flowers choked up,
Her fruit-trees all upturned, her hedges ruin'd,
Her knots disorder'd and her wholesome herbs
Swarming with caterpillars?

Gardener: Hold thy peace:
He that hath suffer'd this disorder'd spring
Hath now himself met with the fall of leaf:
The weeds which his broad-spreading leaves did shelter,
That seem'd in eating him to hold him up
Are pluck'd up root and all by Bolingbroke . . .

Three years after Richard's death his cousin Edmund was also buried at Langley Priory with great ceremony, and then in 1431 the palace was damaged by fire, and although it remained in royal hands until Stuart times, its importance declined and it gradually fell into ruin. The priory, of course, was suppressed by Henry VIII, and the tomb of Edmund, Duke of York, was moved to the parish church, where it can still be seen, adorned with thirteen shields of alabaster. A small part of the priory is all that otherwise survives of princes, priors or palace, and that is incorporated in the buildings of a private school run on the Rudolph Steiner method.

If Kings Langley harbours the rubbish of royalty, the dust of Abbots Langley went to the making of an even more powerful ruler, to whom the parish church here contains a memorial tablet. He was Nicholas Breakspear, born near the neighbouring hamlet of Bedmond. The son of a poor farmer who became a monk at St Albans Abbey, Nicholas himself was refused admission to the monastery and went to France, where he became abbot of a monastery at Avignon, and was then made a cardinal and sent on an important mission to Scandinavia by Pope Eugenius III.

While Nicholas was away, Eugenius died and was succeeded by Anastasius IV, who also died soon after Nicholas's return to Rome. Nicholas, hailed as the "Apostle of the North", was then elected to the papal throne, in 1154. He took the title Adrian IV, and granted some special privileges to the Abbey which had turned him down when a young man. The chief feature of his four years as the prince of Christendom was the growing struggle for supremacy between the Church and the Holy Roman Empire, of which Adrian had crowned Frederick Barbarossa as Emperor in 1155, in secret in St Peter's, and against the wishes of Rome. Adrian died suddenly four years later, in circumstances which, if they were not mysterious then, have become so since. The chronicler of St Albans Abbey, writing a hundred years afterwards, says that Adrian was poisoned, whereas Thomas Fuller, the seventeenth-century historian, suggests (whimsically) that he was choked by a fly. Another, and perhaps more likely, suggestion is that he died of quinsy. At any rate, Abbot's mitre, Cardinal's hat and Pontiff's crown were a hat-trick no other Englishman has performed before or since.

The fertile soil of Abbots Langley was responsible for another remarkable English record, too. Elizabeth Jones, born 1615, married Thomas Greenhill of Hyde Manor, when she was sixteen years old, and bore him thirty-nine children after thirty-eight separate confinements. All their children achieved their majority, and the youngest son, Thomas, became surgeon to the tenth Duke of Norfolk. Mrs Greenhill's husband was secretary to General Monk. She was pregnant every year from the age of sixteen to fifty-four, and died about ten years after her final delivery. One might expect that the local telephone directory would be replete with Greenhills today, but alas, only seven of her enormous progeny were boys.

The parish church at Abbots Langley also contains a monument to Lord Raymond, an eighteenth-century Lord Chief Justice, who is represented with such a smirk of self-satisfaction on his face that one is inclined to take it as a lecherous grin, particularly as the allegorical female figure on his right watches him with a protective hand on her breast.

The famous Ovaltine Egg Farm, familiar to railway passengers on the line through the Langleys, lies close to the Grand Union Canal and the River Gade, beside which, further up the road towards Hemel Hempstead, are the Nash Mill and Apsley Mill of Dickinson's huge paper-making works. The manufacture of paper has been an important business in Hertfordshire for centuries, and indeed the earliest record of a paper mill in England is in a book printed by Caxton in 1495, where John Tate's mill at Hertford is mentioned. The art had taken a long time to reach this island, but it soon became a major industry.

At Frogmore End, just south of the former village of Hemel Hempstead near the present Apsley Mill, two brothers, Henry and Sealy Fourdrinier, together with an engineer, Bryan Donkin, built in 1803 a machine which could make paper by a newly invented French method, in a continuous roll called a web, and the basic principle of this machine is still in use. While the Fourdriniers were building their equipment at Frogmore, a stationer from London bought Apsley Mill and installed Fourdrinier machinery there. His name was John Dickinson. Over the next few years he invented a great many improvements in paper production, including a rival type of machine to the Fourdriniers'. He made paper for cartridges during the Napoleonic Wars, and paper for the first postage stamps. Meanwhile he bought Nash Mill, Home Park Mill at Kings Langley, and Croxley Mill near Watford, and laid the foundations of the huge business Dickinsons has become today. The scattered small paper-making mills in the county, such as at Sarratt and Rickmansworth, gradually closed down in the face of this concentrated mechanical production, and virtually left the field open to Dickinsons.

John Dickinson, a Fellow of the Royal Society, respected as a considerate employer but a trifle eccentric in his private life, built himself a solid house of flint called Abbots Hill, overlooking Nash Mill, and attached an observatory to it so that he could gaze at the moon and stars. It is said that he only used it once. The foundations of the house, which is now a girls' boarding school, consist partly of granite railway sleepers. The bursar kindly showed me round, and told me that the front door, above which a 'D' is cut in stone, is the only door Dickinson allowed in the original house, so that he could keep an eye on what was going on. Some of the original furniture and pictures remain there, but most interesting is the domed observatory, where Dickinson's telescope is still in working order. The views across the Gade valley are no match for the beauty of the cedar trees which Dickinson planted in the grounds.

His daughter, Harriet Ann Dickinson, married her cousin John Evans, the son of the headmaster of Bosworth Grammar School in Leicestershire. John duly became a partner in the firm and was, besides one of the most distinguished scholars of the time, becoming a Fellow of the Royal Society himself and a member of innumerable learned societies. He was also a Doctor of Civil Law, served as a County Councillor and as a Justice of the Peace, and was knighted in 1892 on the recommendation of the Marquis of Salisbury. Sir John's most important contributions to posterity, however, were his book *The Coins of the Ancient Britons* and his son Arthur, who was born at Nash Mills in 1851, and became one of Hertfordshire's most famous men.

Arthur Evans, in his turn, was a brilliant scholar, whose active life in archaeology began when he was the Manchester

Guardian's correspondent in Eastern Europe, and he became curator of the Ashmolean Museum at Oxford when he was thirty-three. Then in 1894 he went to Crete, and his life's work was revealed to him. He began to uncover the remains of the great Minoan civilization and the Palace of Minos at Knossos, with which his name will for ever be linked. In 1908 his father, Sir John Evans, died, and soon afterwards the death of a cousin left Arthur Evans a rich man, the inheritor of the Dickinson estate. His wife had died in 1893 and he was childless. He was free to spend his time and his fortune on continuing his work of discovery, which remains one of the greatest archaeological adventures in history. Evans was knighted in 1911 and died thirty years later, at the age of ninety, with the whole civilized world in his debt.

And so, continuing up the Roman road made when the Palace of Minos was already ancient, we come to Boxmoor and turn off into Hemel Hempstead, and here we have to make a considerable mental adjustment, to switch from one of the earliest civilizations on earth to one of the newest towns in Britain. It will help us to do so, perhaps, if we look briefly at the town's earlier story. Hemel Hempstead grew up as a market town, trading in corn and straw-plaiting, a little north of the junction of the River Bulbourne with the Gade. Chauncy called the Thursday market "one of the greatest for Wheat in this County", and in the eighteenth century it also had a turnover of thousands of pounds a week in straw hats. The town's prosperity is indicated by its parish church of St Mary, mostly of Norman date, with a fine twelfth-century rib-vaulted chancel. Not only is this the only large Norman church in the county except for St Albans Abbey, but it is also one of the very few churches in Hertfordshire with a tall spire; leaded and rising to nearly two hundred feet, between the river and the old High Street.

Richard Field, a notable preacher of Jacobean days, was born here in 1561. The popularity of his sermons drew from King James the comment: "This is indeed a field for God to dwell in!", which shows that royal jokes have not changed much in four hundred years. King Charles felt less inclined to

Devil's Dyke, Wheathampstead

(*above*) The Roman theatre at Verulamium – classical
(*below*) Moor Park near Rickmansworth – neo-classical
(*facing*) Sarratt parish church

Harvesting near Walkern

Old town – Tring

New town – Hemel Hempstead

Riding at Chipperfield

The woods at Ashridge

Friendly ducks and
'Fighting Cocks'

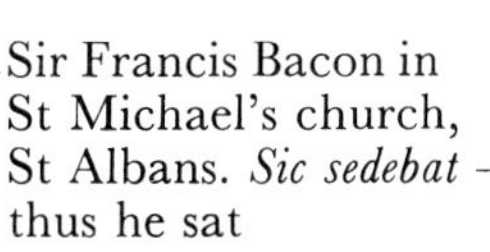

Sir Francis Bacon in St Michael's church, St Albans. *Sic sedebat* – thus he sat

Filming *Spectre* at Elstree Studios. Seated round the table, left to right, are Danny Sturmann (Associate Producer), Gig Young, Ann Bell, Clive Donner (Director), John Hurt, James Villiers

Building Trident aircraft at Hatfield

jest when George Kendall, the vicar of St Mary's, allowed Baptists to preach there, and he was committed to Newgate as a result. Some of Hertfordshire's earliest Dissenters were begat in Hemel, where Luther's doctrines spread, like Wycliffe's, from the Midlands via the Chiltern Hills.

The town was surrounded by meadows which still sport many splendid horse chestnut trees and fine willows along the river banks. A red disc used to be seen on some of the houses in Hemel, which indicated the right of the owner to graze an animal on Roughdown Common at Boxmoor. He could purchase this right for seven shillings and sixpence a year.

Straw-plaiting, which passed over the border to Luton and Dunstable when it became a factory industry, was at one time a very important trade in north and west Hertfordshire. At Hemel Hempstead, Hitchin, Tring, Redbourn and other villages in this area, women and girls could earn a guinea a week, working in their homes at the end of the eighteenth century. They obtained their straw from the markets in bundles supplied by the local farmers, who reaped it for the purpose by hand because machinery broke the stems. The trade was apparently established in this country by James I, who settled French families (brought to Scotland by his mother) under the Napier family at Luton Hoo. Girls were taught how to plait straw at a very early age so that they could contribute to the meagre earnings of poor families.

Hemel Hempstead's old market town character was preserved well into this century by two pieces of good luck. Firstly, the town grew up a mile away from Akeman Street, which in due time became the destructive trunk road it is today. And secondly, when the London and Birmingham Railway was opened in 1837, it came through Boxmoor, following the river valley and the road route, instead of going right into Hemel Hempstead. True, thirty years later the Midland Railway put a line through the town, but that was only a branch line to Harpenden.

After the Second World War, however, this enviable position changed dramatically. Hemel Hempstead was designated one of the New Towns proposed to absorb some of

London's overflowing population, and it began to grow into something very different from its former rural nature. Development began on the eastern side of the town and spread inwards, with an industrial area and new shops and office blocks growing up with the rapidly increasing number of houses and flats. The planned population of the new town in 1949 was 60,000, but this figure has now been overtaken, and growth continues.

However, as one who dislikes large towns intensely, I have to add that the blowing up of Hemel Hempstead has been a very well controlled explosion. There is more to be said about New Towns, inevitably, in later pages of this book, but I may say here that Hemel Hempstead's planning consultant, G. A. Jellicoe, laid the foundations of what has turned out to be the best of the New Towns in Hertfordshire. There is still no major trunk road through it, though the motorway is as close on one side as the A41 on the other; the branch railway was chopped off by the Beeching axe in the 'sixties; and best of all, the old town centre was preserved much as it had been, so that the stylish High Street can still be seen with the church behind it and its attractive brick houses running up the hill and into the countryside. Free and (hitherto) adequate parking space makes the new town centre highly attractive to shoppers, who come from miles away rather than suffer the increasing chaos of Watford and other local centres. However, nothing is perfect. Hemel Hempstead's biggest problem as I write is public concern over its insufficient hospital facilities.

North of the town at Piccott's End there is an old house in which some religious murals were discovered in 1953, dating from the fifteenth century, whilst a little further up the road, Waterend is a delightful hamlet with a little bridge over the stream – a favourite spot with both amateur and professional photographers.

If Hemel Hempstead was fortunate to stand aside and watch the A41 go hurtling past, Berkhamsted stood right in its path and felt the full impact. The wide main street of this old market town, which Leland thought one of the best in Hertfordshire, has become a dreadful thoroughfare now, not only because of the continual traffic, but also because of the weird assortment of modern shopping parades which have gone up along it, although it retains some nice old timbered houses.

I have already mentioned that Saxon noblemen possibly offered William of Normandy the English crown here and the town's history goes back to the Roman occupation. There is even a legend that St Paul came here and drove away serpents and thunderstorms for ever, but nature felt disinclined to obey this apostolic injunction, for the thunderstorms, if not the serpents, have returned. Thomas Becket held the castle here, the remains of which consist merely of the motte and surrounding earthworks. Beyond it, the ground rises to the extensive Common, where a part of that mysterious earthwork Grim's Dyke can be seen. Thought to be a Saxon or earlier boundary line, it begins at Potten End nearby and continues intermittently in a wide arc through the Chilterns towards High Wycombe. The only certainty about it is that it was dug through heavily wooded land when wolves roamed the hills, so it must have been important to those who ordered it, and though it has been variously described as a territorial boundary and a protection against cattle raids, I doubt if the possibility can be entirely ruled out that it was a Belgic line of defence against advancing Roman legions. Those who point out that it was useless as a defensive ditch are right—it was! However much the experts may be baffled by its drawbacks as a military structure, it seems to me that theories about livestock enclosures are even weaker. Marauding wolves must have been a worse menace to farmers than human thieves, and no sort of ditch would have been a defence against *them*.

Berkhamsted's medieval history was moulded by events at the castle, which was originally built by Robert of Mortain, half-brother of William of Normandy. Henry III bestowed the estate, on which Becket had spent a great deal of money, upon his brother Richard, Earl of Cornwall and titular head of the Holy Roman Empire, and he carried out further repairs and extensions, commandeering all the local carts from miles around to carry timber to the site, and causing tradesmen to complain that their businesses were injured as a result. Richard's son Edmund built the monastery at Ashridge, of which more presently. The castle was given to Piers Gaveston by Edward II, and it was there where he married the King's niece. Then Edward III presented it to the Black Prince, who imprisoned King John of France there after Poitiers, and spent his own last years there, dying of an incurable disease contracted during a military expedition in Spain. Geoffrey Chaucer was clerk of works at the castle in Richard II's reign, and although there is no evidence that he ever stayed in or near the castle, the appointment is significant as the first hint of a connection with English literature which Berkhamsted retains.

By Leland's time the castle was "much in ruins", and Sir Edward Cary, Keeper of Jewels to Elizabeth I, finally demolished it and used the materials to build Berkhamsted Place, not far away. Much of the original gabled house was subsequently destroyed by fire, but it was the home for a time of Daniell Axtell, the upstart grocer's boy who became a Colonel in Cromwell's army and stage-managed the trial of Charles I, who had owned Berkhamsted Place before him. At the Restoration, Axtell was executed at Tyburn and his head stuck up like a toffee-apple at Westminster Hall, the scene of his brief entrance on the stage of history. Charles II then gave Berkhamsted Place to his cook, who founded the Sayer Almshouses at the west end of the High Street.

The poor people of Berkhamsted were permitted to take for fuel the wood of the gorse bushes on the extensive Common, but were not allowed to cut any until 1 September. They used to gather on the Common before midnight on 31 August, and as soon as the chimes of the parish church were heard in the distance, they staked their claims to the abundant gold that would keep them warm in the approaching winter.

Berkhamsted gave birth to a Protestant poet and a Catholic novelist of note, one of whom twice attempted to kill himself and the other went through a sort of token suicide. William Cowper was born in 1731, the son of the rector here, and Robert Southey predicted that Berkhamsted would be "more known in after ages as the birthplace of William Cowper than for its connection with so many historical personages who figured in the tragedies of old". Cowper now seems almost a tragedy of old himself, but his reputation as a poet is firmly established.

His mother died when he was six, and as if this were not sufficient trauma for a sensitive child, his father packed him off to school at Markyate where he was mercilessly bullied, and the balance of his mind became extremely fragile. It finally broke down when he was thirty-two. Offered a post as Clerk of Journals to the House of Lords, the growing fear of having to appear before the assembled lords proved too much for him. He became a victim of manic-depression, and twice tried to hang himself. He spent a year in an asylum at St Albans, after which he left Hertfordshire. He called himself "a stricken deer, that left the herd long since" - an image he may well have recalled from a childhood visit to Ashridge Park.

Cowper's poetry forms a link between the classicism of Pope and the naturalism of Wordsworth, and many of his lines have passed into the language, the most frequently misquoted being undoubtedly: "Variety's the very spice of life." Walking, gardening and looking after his tame hares restored this man, who had felt himself damned, to a state of mind in which he could write happily between recurring periods of depression, and perhaps his best-known poem is the amusing story of John Gilpin, "a citizen of credit and renown", who decides with his wife to celebrate their wedding anniversary by riding to the Bell Inn at Edmonton to dine - she in a chaise and he on a borrowed horse. But Gilpin loses control of his steed when it begins to trot, and then it breaks into a mad gallop which only ends when he has passed Edmonton and gone deep into Hertfordshire, and all the way back again:

> Said John - It is my wedding-day,
> And all the world would stare,
> If wife should dine at Edmonton,
> And I should dine at Ware.

Thus the Protestant poet. The Catholic novelist is thankfully still very much alive, and we might venture the thought that Berkhamsted will be more known in after ages as the birthplace of Graham Greene than for its connection with . . . etc. Greene was born in 1904, the son of the headmaster of Berkhamsted School, and he has become one of the most successful and widely read of modern novelists, threading heavy themes of the psychology of guilt, with rare craftsmanship, into action stories generally set in torrid climates. He has related in his autobiography how, at the age of nineteen, he was sufficiently careless of his own life to play Russian Roulette in the woods at Ashridge, and later at Oxford. The exotic locations which journalists delight in calling by the generic term 'Greeneland' are perhaps merely backdrops for the unanswered questions Graham Greene posed for himself in Berkhamsted High Street, trudging "past the town hall, past the new King's Road, up and down which the commuters streamed twice a day to the station with their little attaché cases . . . along the market gardens, with everywhere that odd gritty smell blowing up from the coal yards and the coal barges".

Another author associated with Berkhamsted, though not a native of Hertfordshire, was W. W. Jacobs, who wrote immensely popular humorous stories in his day, but is remembered now chiefly for something very different, the classic horror story 'The Monkey's Paw'.

Sinister undertones were brought to Graham Greene's mind by the name of the inn The Crooked Billet at Northchurch, where he was never taken for a walk as a child; but no half-forgotten happening, whispered about in his hearing by the local people, nor, I believe, any incident conceived in his fertile imagination as a storyteller, could have been more bizarre than the story which ended beneath a gravestone in the churchyard here in 1785. At a farm near Hanover in 1724, a boy of about thirteen was found sucking a cow. He walked like an animal on all fours and ate grass, and was unable to speak. He soon attracted the attention of George I, who brought him to England and kept him at court like a pet dog. He became known as Peter the Wild Boy, and excited the curiosity of, among others, Dean Swift, who ought to have known better. For if the boy was an imbecile, that was hardly worse than the King, who was very stupid; and if the only thing that impressed him was music, that was a taste he shared with the King; and if he spoke not a word of English, well neither did the King of England. Unfortunately, however, as Queen Caroline soon discovered, so far was Peter from speaking any English that he could not be taught to speak any human language at all, and the court lost interest in him. He was then farmed out to a man named Fenn at Northchurch, on an allowance of thirty-five pounds a year. And here Peter spent the rest of his long life with an inscribed leather collar round his neck, in case he wandered off, which said: "Peter the Wild Man from Hanover, whoever will bring him to Mr. Fenn, at Berkhamsted, Hertfordshire, shall be paid for their trouble."

A road from Northchurch leads across Berkhamsted Common and up to the Ashridge estate, now largely owned by the National Trust, and one of the most popular local destinations for weekend motorists - a pilgrimage for town-dwellers ostensibly seeking the country air, though when they arrive there they remain in or near their cars; parties to a national conspiracy to drug the very atmosphere with petrol fumes. Ashridge was a place of pilgrimage from its earliest days, but with a very different object.

Richard, Earl of Cornwall, returning to England a hero of the Crusades, brought with him to Berkhamsted, according to Holinshed, a golden box containing what was said to be blood from the body of Christ, and in 1276 his son Edmund founded a religious house on the clay plateau here where the coagulated souvenir, the authenticity of which had been reverently confirmed by the Patriarch of Jerusalem, could be preserved.

The monastery was built of Totternhoe stone, and Edmund imported a group of Augustinian monks of the Order of Bonhommes from France, who were left to their devotions among the Chiltern beech woods for 250 years, whilst the monastery became wealthy. The Black Prince, dying at the castle, endowed the monastery with riches which included "a great table of gold and silver, all full of precious relics . . . garnished with stones and pearls, that is to say twenty-five rubies, thirty-four sapphires, fifteen great pearls and several other sapphires, emeralds and little pearls, to the High Altar of our House at Ashridge".

As well as the devout who came to the monastery, however, princes came to hunt deer in the park, and when the monastery was suppressed and the gory relic exposed as a fake, Henry VIII took Ashridge for himself. The monastery register recorded the date in 1535: "This year the noble house of Asscherugge was destroyed and brethren driven out on St Leonard's Day" – 6 November. In 1550 it became the property of Henry's daughter by Ann Boleyn, the auburn-haired Lady Elizabeth, who divided her time between Ashridge and Hatfield until Mary Tudor, suspecting her half-sister's implication in plots to overthrow her, had Elizabeth taken from Ashridge to the Tower. Elizabeth leased Ashridge in 1556 and never returned there.

After the Queen's death, the property was bought by her Lord Keeper of the Seal, Sir Thomas Egerton, whose descendants became the Earls of Bridgewater; the fourth Earl, who married the Duke of Marlborough's daughter, was made a Duke by George I. It was his grandson Francis, the third Duke, who allowed the house to fall into ruin and thus brought about the building we see today. Francis Egerton inherited Ashridge and the title at the age of twelve. He grew up to be a man of enormous size and imperceptible intellect, a notorious woman-hater whom the locals were apt to regard, with some justification, as "a proper wicked old buguer". Notwithstanding this, however, Ashridge has a tall monument to him, on account of his having become famous as the 'father of Inland Navigation'. He built one of the country's first industrial canals, to convey coal from his Lancashire mines to Manchester.

After his death, his cousin the seventh Earl employed James Wyatt to rebuild Ashridge, and the old monastery buildings were soon demolished. Wyatt, known as 'The Destroyer' in recognition of his 'restoration' of various cathedrals, was a specialist in the sham-Gothic style of architecture, and at Ashridge he composed a solemn Mass, impressive to catholic tastes but abhorrent to purists. Pevsner calls it 'spectacular'. H. J. Massingham likened it to a wedding cake. It is a pile of pointed windows, pinnacles and crenellated towers, surmounted by a recent spire made of fibreglass and lowered into position by helicopter! But Wyatt's chapel is undeniably impressive, as is the Main Hall, with its high fan-vaulted roof, and a staircase taking the eye at first-floor level to nine statues set round the walls in canopied niches.

The property passed in due course to the Earls Brownlow, and it was the second of these who created a local *cause célèbre* when he attempted to enclose part of Berkhamsted Common and add it to his deer park. A gang of navvies enlisted in London was brought up by train and pulled up all the fences during the night, and the case went to court, where it stayed four years, eventually ending in judgement for the traditional commoners' rights. Lord Brownlow was dead by that time.

When the estate was sold to meet death duties, following the death of the third Earl, a large part of it, extending into Buckinghamshire, was acquired by the National Trust, and a local committee now runs it and keeps it tidy – a formidable task when one sees the rubbish dumped there by civilized England on its days off. But there are some very delightful walks in the woods and commons away from the congregation of vehicles, and in the autumn, the dazzling spectacle of copper and cinnamon, green and gold, red and rust, scarlet and saffron, must surely have worked its sensuous magic on fourteenth-century saints as effectively as on twentieth-century sinners.

John Skelton, Henry VIII's court poet, wrote of this place:

> Of the bone homs at Ashridge beside Barcamstede,
> That goodly place to Skelton most kynde,
> Where the sange royall is, Christis blood so rede,
> Whereupon he metrified after his mynde,
> A pleasanter place than Ashridge is harde were to finde.

The house itself became a College of Citizenship for the Conservative Party, and then a Management College for industry, which is its role today. It is opened to the public on a limited number of days each year.

Ashridge is in the parish of Little Gaddesden, and in the church of Saints Peter and Paul is a series of monuments to the Earls of Bridgewater and other members of the Egerton family. The eighth and last Earl never owned Ashridge. He was the Rev. Francis Egerton, sometime rector of Whitchurch in Shropshire and later resident in Paris. If his particular brand of Egerton eccentricity had stopped at preferring the company of dogs to that of human beings, it would have been no more than a peculiarity shared with a lot of Englishmen; but this reverend gentleman's contributions to the spiritual well-being of mankind included dressing up his dogs and having them seated at the dinner table to be served by his liveried flunkeys. There is also a monument to Elizabeth, the daughter of the Duke of Marlborough, who married Scroop Egerton, the fourth Earl and first Duke of Bridgewater, and who died of smallpox.

Little Gaddesden was the home of a witch named Rosina Massey, who was apt to fly through the air towards Studham, and was reputed to have done a local man to death. Her three-legged stool was seen by imaginative villagers, on occasions, running errands for her.

This village was also the home of William Ellis, a noted eighteenth-century writer on agriculture and local customs, who gives us, among other things, a recipe for cherry cordial:

> Pack ripe pick'd black Kerroon Cherries in a Jar, or earthen glazed Pot, with white Sugar, by first putting a Layer of Sugar about half an Inch thick, then a Layer of Cherries, next a thinner Layer of Sugar, then Cherries, and so on till the Pot is full: Then put a half Pint of clean old Molasses Brandy, or better French Brandy, into a Gallon Pot of them; cover them close, and bury deep enough in the Ground from the Power of the Frost. After three or more Months Time, you may take up the Pot, and I will answer for it you will find an excellent rich Cordial indeed, surpassing most others.

The people of the hamlet of Frithsden nearby (pronounced Freezeden) were nicknamed 'Cherry Pickers' and a field there is still called Cherry Bounce. It also has a lane to Nettleden called Spooky Lane, flanked by brick and flint walls and dark with overhanging trees, passing under a bridge carrying an overgrown track without a destination. You can feel the temperature drop as you walk into its dip. I would advise explorers to enter it from the Frithsden end, as the effect is better, and the climb from the Nettleden end is deceptively steep.

On the opposite side of the Ashridge estate is Aldbury, one of Hertfordshire's most attractive villages, though to my mind the stocks and whipping post beside the pond, far from being 'quaint', are ghastly survivals of a crueller England, and should be viewed as such. The stocks inspired the name of a large old house outside the village, which was the home of the Victorian novelist Mrs Humphry Ward whose first book *Robert Elsmere* became famous for its sensational attack on evangelical Christianity. Mrs Ward was one of the first women magistrates, but was fiercely opposed to the suffragette movement. She was the niece of Matthew Arnold, mother-in-law of the historian G. M. Trevelyan, and aunt of Julian and Aldous Huxley, who often visited her here. Aldous said she was a "kind of literary godmother" to him.

Near Aldbury is Tring Station, where the railway line enters Hertfordshire through a long and deep cutting to converge with road, river and canal in the Tring Gap, where all four pass through the Chilterns and then keep together all the way to Watford. It is time we looked a little more closely at the Grand Union Canal.

It began as the Grand Junction Canal, and was part of a long-term plan to link the Trent with the Thames, so that coal and other freight could be carried to London from the Midlands and the north. William Jessop was its chief engineer, and the Earls of Clarendon and Essex among its supporters, having given permission (for a consideration) for the canal to pass through Grove Park and Cassiobury Park respectively. Work began in 1793 from both ends. By 1796 the southern work had reached Hemel Hempstead and three years later it reached Tring. The whole canal was open for traffic by 1805, and a good many of its 101 locks were in the hilly country of west Hertfordshire. Jessop had pointed out at an early stage that the high ground at Tring was one of the major engineering problems of the whole project, and the reservoirs north of the town were built to supply water to the canal, which is nearly 400 feet above sea level at this point. Pumping became necessary there, and in times of drought the passage of barges was reduced to such an extent that long queues formed along the banks.

Lords Clarendon and Essex subsequently had a difference of opinion over canal operations. Lord Clarendon objected to the navigation of boats on Sundays, but Lord Essex protested that "lawless, ignorant and untractable men" would commit acts of "depredation, drunkenness and riot" if not kept fully occupied. John Dickinson also fell out with the canal company over the water-power needed for his mills, and the issue was speedily resolved to his satisfaction, as he supplied the canal with a good deal of valuable trade. By this time, however, the threat of the coming railway was reducing the value of canal shares, and when the railway was in full operation, the canal's failure to compete led to an amalgamation of canal companies between London and the Midlands, resulting in the renaming of the Grand Junction as the Grand Union Canal.

The Tring reservoirs, now nature reserves, lie in a peninsular part of Hertfordshire occupied at its furthest extremity by Puttenham and Long Marston, the latter being a pleasant old village at its centre, though spoiled elsewhere by the shapeless spread of modern dwellings. The roads near these villages boast frequent humpback bridges as they cross the canals at various points.

The hamlet of Gubblecote, near Long Marston, was the scene of a notorious crime in 1751 when an elderly couple, John and Ruth Osborn, were the victims of mob violence. Another famous case in Hertfordshire, to which we shall come in due course, had brought about the Act of Parliament which abolished the death penalty for witches, in 1735.

But Thomas Colley, a chimney sweep, was the chief instigator of a popular clamour against this couple - both over seventy - who were supposed to have bewitched a local farm, and a mob set about exacting its own vengeance. The old couple hid in the vestry of the church, but were dragged out, stripped naked, tied together and dragged through a pond. The woman was dead when she was pulled out, and the man died soon afterwards.

Colley was tried at Hertford Assizes for wilful murder and condemned to death. Hanged at Wilstone Green, his body was hung in chains on a gibbet, where it remained rotting away for years, and it was said that a great black dog - Colley's disembodied spirit - haunted the scene long afterwards. One can only say of all this that the law was as ignorant as the mob, and the punishment as grotesque as the crime.

Tring is an ancient market town, and its market was noted particularly at one time for the fine veal on sale there, from which the local people made minced veal pies. The town was diverted from its original position on the Roman Akeman Street by Sir William Gore, a Lord Mayor of London and Director of the Bank of England, who acquired Tring Park and disliked the road running through it. Roman roads went in straight lines regardless of obstacles, but the modern A41 has a winding course through Tring and became such a bottleneck that a motorway diversion has had to be created, putting the trunk road more or less back to where it was in the first place! The ancient Icknield Way, however, which passes by on its way south-west to Wendover, is probably of greater significance in the early history of Tring than the Roman road.

The first house at Tring Park was designed by Sir Christopher Wren for Sir Henry Guy, Secretary of the Treasury, who, according to Defoe, ran into frequent trouble with the poor of the parish over their rights of commonage when he tried to enclose Wigginton Common to form his park. Charles II visited this house and so, it is fondly imagined, did Nell Gwynne.

Sir William Gore died in 1707 and his impressive

monument, presumed to be by a pupil of Grinling Gibbons, dominates the parish church. After the Gore family, the mansion was bought by Baron Lionel de Rothschild, who rebuilt it, and his descendants did much good in the town, where they are remembered gratefully. It is recorded, however, that one bishop took a dim view of the local parson consorting with Jews, to which the parson retorted: "But my Lord, I have great hopes of converting them."

The second Baron Rothschild, a Fellow of the Royal Society, stocked Tring Park with a vast collection of animals and birds, and was apt to drive down the High Street in a carriage drawn by zebras – an amiable eccentricity. It was he, of course, who founded the Tring Museum which is now part of the Natural History Section of the British Museum. It contains millions of preserved specimens of animals, birds, fish and insects, though not including the victims of a wholesale slaughter by Edward VII and his party during a stay with Lord Rothschild in 1897, when 500 wild ducks, 200 coot "and a few extras" were shot.

Destruction had been part of the way of life in this district for centuries, however, working its way into the collective unconscious of the people. North-east of the old Tring, in the fourteenth century, there was a village of some size called Pendley, in which "divers handicraftsmen, as tailors, shoemakers and cardmakers" lived. But about 1440 Sir Robert Whittingham obtained a licence to enclose 200 acres there. He pulled down the houses, seized the tenants' land, and built a mansion on the site with pasture-land for his livestock, and the people for whom the village had been home saw it disappear as they moved elsewhere; early victims of an impersonal process known today as a 'compulsory purchase order' when land is required by the ruling powers for motorways, airports and nuclear power stations. Pendley Manor is now an adult education centre, but has been the home for many years of the Williams family, lords of the manor of Pendley, whose present representative is Dorian Williams, the well-known horseman and commentator.

At least two other villages have disappeared from the Tring

peninsula. Tiscott and Betlow lay at the furthest extremity of this part of the county, beyond Long Marston. Betlow Farm remains, between a disused railway cutting and a long line of cable-carrying pylons. Were the villages total casualties of the Black Death? We do not know, but the A41, which has carried us, like a strong current, through this western side of the county, leaves it just beyond a cemetery at Tring, and death awaits us at our next point of entry, also.

III

THE WAY TO THE STARS

WATLING STREET, the most famous of Britain's Roman roads, steers a somewhat uncertain course through Hertfordshire these days, as if it has lost the sense of direction it possessed to a marked degree when it was first made. The military audacity which laid it in a straight line nearly two thousand years ago, from Dover towards Chester, has recently lost some of the awesome respect it once commanded, and practical necessity has rerouted the road in certain places, so that it now takes, for instance, an eccentric turn into the centre of St Albans, and then swerves off course like a drunken driver between Flamstead and Markyate, after which it resumes its arrow-like course towards Dunstable and the Midlands.

It enters the county at Elstree, the name of which is of doubtful origin, having been spelt as variously as Heaghstre and Idlestree in times past. Nor was it mentioned in Domesday Book, but at a later date the parish was large enough to include the hamlet of Barham or Borehamwood – waste ground in the nineteenth century. The 'hamlet' has now far outgrown the village, which stands on high ground overlooking the Aldenham Reservoir. The steep climb out of Edgware, up Brockley Hill and past the Aldenham Bus Works, brings you into Elstree near streets with promising names like Beethoven Road, Schubert Road and Elgar Close, but unfortunately, you do not enter Hertfordshire until you pass the traffic lights – a trio of more prosaic orchestration. Some say that the undiscovered Roman city of Sullonicae was where Elstree now stands. Neither Elstree nor Borehamwood is a pretty place today, but Borehamwood, with its large industrial estate, has all the drawbacks of a rapidly developed new town without any of the virtues of an officially designated 'New Town'.

Drama in various guises seems to have latched on to the parish of Elstree. That colourful character Sir Richard Burton, traveller, linguist and translator of the Arabian Nights, was born here, and William Macready, the great tragic actor, lived here, the unvanquished king of the British stage until Borehamwood came to Dunsinane, as it were, and the end of Macbeth closed his career in 1851.

I said that death awaited us at Elstree, and so it does, in no small measure. This village was the birthplace of Martha Ray, the mistress of the Earl of Sandwich, and she was shot dead outside Covent Garden Theatre by a clergyman, one James Hackman, who had fallen in love with her many years before but had been continually repulsed. He claimed that until the last second he had intended only to kill himself in front of her. James Boswell, who attended the subsequent trial, relates that Dr Johnson was of the opinion that Hackman had intended to kill the woman as well as himself, as he had taken two pistols with him. At any rate, the clergyman was hanged at Tyburn.

This case was incidental to Elstree, but one which concerned the village more directly was the notorious Gills Hill Murder of 1823, which the Press of the time exploited for all it was worth. The case became known as "the Elstree murder", but in fact it was committed at Radlett, which was a tiny hamlet then. As the body was found at Elstree, which was better known, that village gave its name to the crime. One of the popular ballads of the day called it, more appropriately, "The Hertfordshire Tragedy". The trial has some serious significance in the history of Hertfordshire, apart from the sensationalism surrounding the case, because it was the last trial in England conducted under the Tudor procedure whereby an accused man had to defend himself during inquisition by his accusers.

John Thurtell was the son of a Mayor of Norwich. He fell in with a gang of low sporting types and decided to kill William Weare, a solicitor, apparently because the latter had cheated him in a game of billiards. Weare having accepted an invitation to spend a weekend at the cottage of Thurtell's crony, William Probert, in Gills Hill Lane, Thurtell travelled with him in a gig from London, and on arrival at Radlett, suddenly pulled out a pistol and fired point blank at Weare's face, but the bullet glanced off his cheekbone. Thurtell then fell upon his terrified victim and cut his throat with a penknife. He then rammed the barrel of his pistol at Weare's head with such violence that it penetrated the skull and filled the barrel with blood and tissue. Meanwhile, Probert and another crony, Joseph Hunt, had turned up, and they dumped Weare's body in a pond in the garden until later, when they took it to another pond at Elstree. But some labourers at Radlett soon found the bloody pistol and penknife which Thurtell had carelessly dropped, and a major murder hunt was in progress in no time. When two Bow Street runners questioned Probert, he immediately offered to turn King's evidence before Hunt, who was a professional singer, had the chance, though Hunt hastily showed them where the body was.

The trial at Hertford Assizes was before Mr Justice Park, whose chief claim to immortality was his question to a small girl on another occasion when he was trying to ascertain her Christian virtue and capacity to give evidence: "What do you do, my little maid," he said, "just before you get into bed?" The little maid, with some show of embarrassment, gave him a more honest answer than he had bargained for. The trial of Thurtell and Hunt (as an accessory before the fact) concentrated the minds of the whole country on Hertfordshire for a time, and stage plays, ballads and many books were written about the case; the guilt of Thurtell being so generally assumed by the Press that the judge was led to remark that if "these statements of evidence before trial which corrupt the purity of the administration of justice in its source . . . are not checked, I tremble for the fate of our country".

Thurtell's speech in his own defence was a long and rambling mixture of emotional blackmail and dubious argument, which has impressed commentators as being exceptionally eloquent, for some unaccountable reason. Perhaps they were carried away by the circumstance that the defendant was, at any rate, literate. "My lord," Thurtell began, "and you, gentlemen of the jury, under the pressure of greater difficulties than perhaps it has ever before fallen to the lot of man to sustain, I now appear before you to vindicate my character and preserve my life." But in the face of his obvious guilt, it is questionable whether some of Thurtell's remarks were best calculated to vindicate his character: ". . . calumniated and charged as I am," he said, "what bosom can refuse a sigh? What eye can deny a tear?" He explained that he was reared by "a kind, affectionate, and religious mother, who taught my lips to utter their first accents in praise of that Being who guides the conduct of your hearts and of the learned judge upon the bench". He then proceeded, with true Christian feeling, to accuse Probert of being the real murderer, and called upon the words of Voltaire, the Apostle Paul, and the Newgate Calendar in his defence – a mixed bag of witnesses which did not unduly impress Mr Justice Park, who commented that the Newgate Calendar, "for anything I know to the contrary, may be mere books of romance".

Whatever effect Thurtell's speech may have had on the jury, the judge's summing-up was lengthy enough to deaden it, and the twelve good men and true needed only twenty minutes to find Thurtell and Hunt guilty. Both were sentenced to death, Thurtell's body to be given, after hanging, to the surgeons for dissection. He was hanged in front of Hertford Gaol by Tom Cheshire, known as 'Old Cheese', who – as was the custom with executioners – got thoroughly drunk the night before, telling stories of his experiences in return for free drinks, but he hanged his 'party' so efficiently next morning that Thurtell's neck broke "with a sound like a pistol shot". Hunt's sentence was commuted to transportation, and he lived to old age at Botany Bay. Probert got his comeuppance in the following year when he was hanged for stealing a horse.

All this real-life drama in Elstree's history had nothing to do with its becoming a centre of the British motion-picture industry in this century, though it seems singularly appropriate that it should have done so. I should point out, however, that as Elstree gave its name to a murder committed at Radlett, so it also gave its name to film studios which were, in fact, at Borehamwood.

The earliest studio there was in operation by 1908, and there were half a dozen small studios soon after the First World War. The original so-called Elstree Studios were built by an American, J. D. Williams, who appointed Herbert Wilcox as director-in-chief, but they were taken over by John Maxwell, who formed British International Pictures in 1926. The studios were the most modern and well-equipped in Britain, and the first capable of producing sound pictures. Alfred Hitchcock's *Blackmail* was in effect the first British talkie, made at Elstree in 1929. Maxwell's set-up became, in due course, the Associated British Picture Corporation, and when he made an offer to purchase the nearby Amalgamated Studios, J. Arthur Rank moved in to thwart him.

Metro-Goldwyn-Mayer was the first American company to take an active interest in British film production, and its studios at Borehamwood made *The Citadel* and *Goodbye Mr Chips*, which both starred the courageous Robert Donat. But M.G.M. closed down when war broke out in 1939, and after the war, the Hungarian Alexander Korda reopened the studios as M.G.M.-London Films whilst, on the death of Maxwell in 1941, Warner Brothers bought a large interest in the A.B.P.C.

Korda employed his brothers Vincent and Zoltan at Elstree, and Emlyn Williams has described how he and Robert Donat passed time between takes inventing new relations for the maestro, such as Sash Korda, Miseri Korda and Umbilical Korda. Donat and Williams were later to work together on the film made at Elstree for the Festival of Britain, called *The Magic Box* and dealing with the invention of the cinematograph by William Friese-Green. It was one of the sadder adventures of the British film industry, assembling an impressive supporting cast (Olivier, Ustinov, Redgrave) to celebrate a non-event, for Friese-Green was not, in fact, the inventor of the cinematograph, but merely one of those in the race to perfect it.

One of Hertfordshire's native personalities in the film industry was Frank Launder, who was born at Hitchin. He formed his own production company in partnership with Sidney Gilliatt, and the two wrote the script of Hitchcock's film *The Lady Vanishes*, while Launder himself directed *The Blue Lagoon* and the *St Trinians* films.

In the troubled times the industry has gone through since the rise of television, the entertainment factories at Borehamwood have shared the decline of the other British studios. Now district councils, engineers and a cold storage firm inhabit the various studios where actors, designers, make-up artists, wardrobe mistresses, cameramen, script-writers, musicians, lighting technicians, carpenters, stunt-men and directors, to mention but a few, have combined their talents to produce the fantasies which have insulated our consciousness for brief periods against the shocking current of reality.

The large old M.G.M. studios finally closed in 1970, but production continues at the A.B.P. lot, now part of the huge E.M.I. organization, where films such as *The Dambusters*, *Moby Dick* and *The Avengers* T.V. series were made. These studios were losing a million pounds a year before the present director took charge of them as the most up-to-date facility studios in the country.

The film industry at Borehamwood is an important part of modern Hertfordshire's story, but it requires a book of its own to do it full justice, and we must be content to note here that legendary directors, cameramen and stars have worked in this corner of the county to make films which have, on occasion, risen above the practical purposes of entertainment and dollar-earning and achieved something more – status as works of art. Great actors such as Laurence Olivier, Charles Laughton, Orson Welles, Alec Guinness and Edith Evans have worked here, as well as comedians such as Will Hay, Tony Hancock and Peter Sellers, glamorous stars such as Maureen O'Hara and Ursula Andress, and directors from Alfred Hitchcock to Ken Russell. Russell had said that he would not make another film at Elstree Studios, after the sets collapsed while he was making *The Boy Friend* in 1971, but he is back there as I write, faithful to the showbiz motto "the show must go on", making a film about Rudolf Valentino, who died in 1926, the year in which the first film was made at Elstree Studios.

The Mops and Brooms public house, near the former M.G.M. studios, is said to be named after traditional fights between local people and groups of gypsies who camped on Rowley Green, the gypsies having regularly brought the wares they sold into service as weapons on these occasions.

Radlett is barely mentioned in most of the pre-1945 guides to Hertfordshire, although the Midland Railway was built through it in 1868. The *Victoria County History* was still able to describe it in 1908 as a hamlet, and Pevsner's few lines on the village single out mainly the oddly-shaped road house built in 1935 as The House Boat, near the northern extremity of Radlett's creep along Watling Street, and now the British Physical Laboratories. Radlett does, however, have the unusual Hertfordshire distinction of a church with a broach spire.

Radlett was once owned by Walter Phillimore, a wealthy Liberal lord and friend of Gladstone, and he passed it on to his son Bobby who was, according to Bertrand Russell, the original of the poet Marchbanks in Shaw's *Candida*. He proceeded to develop Radlett by putting up, in Russell's words, "vast numbers of cheap, ugly, sordid suburban villas, which brought in an enormous profit". Now, twenty minutes from St Pancras, Radlett is a favourite and expensive – though nondescript – commuter centre.

To the east of this village lies Shenley, the name of which is inseparable, in most local people's minds, from its large mental hospital occupying what was formerly Porter's Park, the home of the architect Nicholas Hawksmoor, who died there in 1736. It was also the home of Admiral Lord Howe.

Across the A5 from Shenley, Garston – described by Cussans as "a small hamlet sparsely scattered on both sides of St Albans Road" – has since been completely swamped by Watford, which also threatens to consume Bricket Wood. Although the latter is in the St Albans parish of St Stephen, it is separated from Garston now only by the M1 motorway, and was once a large common and wood where the River Ver joins the Colne. On the west side of the motorway the grounds of a crematorium sport a fine display of rhododendrons in the spring.

On the other side of the road, the extensive Building Research Station carries out government research on structural methods and materials. This establishment was founded in 1921, and moved four years later to its present site, the estate known as Bucknalls, where Lieutenant-Colonel Henry Creed had built himself a sizeable but undistinguished house in 1855. This was bought by the Crown in 1924 and is still standing, though used as offices and surrounded by the Building Research Establishment's newer buildings and developments. The Fire Research Station at Borehamwood is also part of the establishment, which now operates under the Department of the Environment, and employs well over a thousand people. It was the first such organization in the world, and is still the largest of its kind.

One could pick on almost any aspect of building to which the Building Research Station has contributed valuable research during its existence – the durability of bricks; the heating of schools; the lighting of hospitals; the design of tall buildings; the effects of fire on plastics – but one that interested me, and which may seem less obvious, was the experimentation that led to improvement in the acoustics of the Royal Festival Hall.

The quality of sound in a large hall is related to its volume in proportion to the number of seats, and when some doubts about the hall's acoustics were voiced by critics a few years after it had been built, the Greater London Council asked the Building Research Station what could be done to improve the hall, short of making the roof higher, which would have involved enormous cost, or reducing the number of seats, which would have been economically absurd. The answer was provided by a B.R.S. scientist, Peter Parkin, whose invention of "assisted resonance" won him an award for what was described as "a unique example in the field of scientific contribution to the arts"; the Festival Hall's acoustics having since been generally recognized as the finest in the world.

The hamlets of Colney Street, Frogmore and Park Street were strung out along the road towards St Albans until 1859, when they were united into a single parish with its church at Frogmore, an unimpressive early work of Sir George Gilbert Scott. Now running the total length of the three hamlets alongside the road is the Radlett aerodrome, its deserted runways sprouting weeds between the cracks in the concrete, and its remaining buildings housing publishers and furniture manufacturers. For this was the home of Handley Page, the last of the private aircraft companies, which went bankrupt at the end of the 'sixties.

If men such as Rank, Korda and Wilcox made a part of this county into a land of make-believe, it was Sir Frederick Handley Page who made Hertfordshire a land fit for aeros. Born in 1885, he entered the aircraft industry in 1908, forming a company at Barking to build aeroplanes designed by others, but he soon produced successful designs of his own, and built the R.A.F.'s earliest multi-engined heavy bombers in the First World War. In 1919 he ran the first regular commercial services between London and Paris, and five years later formed Imperial Airways by merging Handley Page Transport with other companies. Handley Page's Hannibal four-engined biplane made its first flight from Radlett in 1930, shortly after the company moved there from Cricklewood, and entered service with Imperial Airways in the following year, bringing improved standards of comfort to air travel.

It was during the Second World War that Handley Page Ltd made its greatest contribution to British aircraft design, when the Halifax heavy bomber came into service in 1941, and made the first daylight raids on Germany. Together with the Avro Lancaster, the Halifax formed the backbone of Bomber Command's heavy mob. Radlett airfield was enlarged to help the output of the bombers, and among other premises requisitioned to aid production were the M.G.M. film studios at Borehamwood. Handley Page built six thousand of these aircraft, and their seven-man R.A.F. crews flew on well over eighty thousand operations.

After the war, Handley Page successfully entered the jet age, but Sir Frederick died in 1962, mercifully before the growing troubles of the aircraft industry led to the bankruptcy of his pioneering company. The Jetstream light transport aircraft, which made its first flight at Radlett in 1967, was the last Handley Page aeroplane seen regularly over Hertfordshire. Sir Frederick – a genial but resolute individualist – had resisted pressure from the Government to amalgamate with one of the larger manufacturing groups. In the late 'sixties, the company had hopes of orders which would have kept the firm going, but these failed to materialize, and the company was placed in the hands of a receiver. For many months a number of Handley Page Victor bombers could be seen lined up on the Radlett airfield for reservicing, but in March 1970 the company was finally wound up, its employees sent home, and its outstanding work passed to Hawker-Siddeley.

The course of the original Roman road beyond Park Street continues today only as far as St Stephen's Church in St Albans. It once went straight across where the King Harry public house stands, and through Verulamium, via the site of St Michael's Church, past the theatre and alongside the River Ver, rejoining the present road near Bow Bridge. Now, it takes a most un-Roman turn into St Albans, which would undoubtedly be better off without it.

As the history of Verulamium and St Albans has played such a major part in shaping Hertfordshire, and as St Albans sits somewhat uncomfortably astride both A5 and A6, the ancient and modern cities deserve a chapter of their own, but we might pause here to look at Gorhambury, which lies to the west of Verulamium, and brings to our notice one of the greatest figures connected with Hertfordshire, though not – as is sometimes said – a native, for both Francis Bacon and his father Nicholas were born in London.

Sir Nicholas Bacon, Queen Elizabeth's Lord Keeper of the Great Seal, was related by marriage to William Cecil, Lord Burghley, and by this marriage he had two sons, Anthony and Francis. Sir Nicholas built Gorhambury in 1568 (Francis was seven years old then), and the Queen visited the house twice, remarking on the first occasion: "My Lord, what a little house you have gotten." She also met Francis later at Cambridge, and was sufficiently impressed by his intellect to call him her "young Lord Keeper", but on the death of Sir Nicholas, which threw Francis on his own resources, she declined to help him, despite a plea from his new ally, the Earl of Essex, who eventually presented Bacon with an estate at Twickenham.

In 1601 Francis's older brother Anthony died and he inherited Gorhambury, to which he made some alterations. In the same year Essex, having fallen out of the Queen's favour and raised his rebellion, was charged with treason, and Bacon, among those appointed to investigate the causes of the revolt, proceeded with indecent haste to secure his former friend's conviction, and Essex was beheaded. This event has led to Bacon's being branded as a monster of treachery and ingratitude, and Pope called him "the wisest, brightest, meanest of mankind".

In 1606 he married, for money, Alice Barnham, the daughter of a rich merchant. Their life together was not altogether happy, and Alice could not get on with Francis's mother, Lady Anne, who continued to live at Gorhambury. But from that time, following the accession of James I, whom Bacon had flattered rather fulsomely in *The Advancement of Learning*, Francis rose to great power and influence, becoming Solicitor General, then Attorney-General, then Lord Keeper like his father, and then Lord Chancellor as Baron Verulam, and in 1621, he was made Viscount St Albans, and lived in such style that, as John Aubrey put it, "St Albans seemed as if the Court were there".

Then, in the same year, Bacon was suddenly charged with accepting bribes and brought before the House of Lords, to whom he confessed that he had been guilty of corruption and neglect, but denied that justice had been perverted by the bribes he had taken, leaving us to conclude that he treated those from whom he accepted gifts in the same contemptuous way as he had treated Essex. He was deprived of his offices, sent to the Tower for as long as it was the King's pleasure to keep him there, and fined £40,000. In fact, the King freed him after only four days and the fine was remitted, and Bacon then devoted his remaining five years to literature and learning.

Modern writers anxious to assert Bacon's high standing in the history of the intellect have tended to excuse his behaviour on the grounds that he lived in a corrupt society in which bribery, favouritism and treachery were normal ingredients in the successes of ambitious men. But no amount of argument can turn Bacon into a virtuous man. He was extravagant and wildly incompetent in the management of his affairs, and he died leaving enormous debts, unpaid servants and frustrated executors unable to discharge their duties.

We like our images of men to be simple and straightforward in England. We do not easily embrace opposing characteristics in one person, and would prefer to be told that Bacon was either a great man or a wicked scoundrel. But the facts deny us such simplicity. His moral stature was no better, and somewhat worse, than that of his contemporaries, but Bacon's intellect has been admired for three and a half centuries, the envy of smaller fry. He is claimed by philosophers as the father of the inductive method of philosophy, and by scientists as the father of the experimental method of science, and indeed, although he was sufficiently a child of his time to dismiss the discoveries made by telescopes as due to flaws in the lens, he died after catching a chill whilst stuffing a chicken with snow, to test his idea that low temperature might arrest the decay of food – a thought for which Americans are so grateful, it would seem, that they are constantly trying to reward him with the authorship of Shakespeare's plays.

Gorhambury passed to Sir Thomas Meautys, Bacon's cousin and secretary, and it was he who erected the famous life-size monument of marble in St Michael's Church, where Bacon is supposed, uncertainly, to be buried. This sculpture is one of the most remarkable works of art in the county, being very unusual in style for its date. Unfortunately we do not know the artist responsible for it. Later the estate was sold to Sir Harbottle Grimston, who became Speaker of the House of

Commons and married Meautys's widow, Ann Bacon, the daughter of Sir Nathaniel Bacon the painter. In 1777 the Grimstons, by then Earls of Verulam, built a new mansion designed by Sir Robert Taylor, and the Gorhambury of Francis Bacon fell into ruin.

Redbourn, where the River Ver rises and gives the name meaning 'reed stream' to the village, further up Watling Street, grew up around the village church and the prehistoric earthworks known as The Aubreys, but gradually moved east to benefit from the trade available on the main road. Now Watling Street has become such an embarrassment to it that the villagers want a bypass, since they can scarcely cross the road without putting their lives in jeopardy.

The earliest mention of cricket in Hertfordshire relates to Redbourn Common in 1666, and races and cockfighting were also held there. The first week in January was the date of a big fair at Redbourn, when horses, cattle and sheep were sold, and the horses were tethered to rings in the garden wall of Cumberland House, built in 1745. No doubt Mary Lofty did a roaring trade during Fair week. The Bull Inn was an important staging post in coaching days, and Mary Lofty was an elderly widow well known for her alacrity in collecting horse dung after coaches had passed by, and selling it to local farmers, by which means she earned a sufficient living in days when there were no pensions.

The way to the stars was rather less clearly marked for a vicar of Redbourn than for others in the vicinity of Watling Street. Lord Frederick Beauclerk was a sporting parson whose parish clerk was liable to announce to the congregation, during the hunting season, that the vicar would be going to follow the Leicestershire hounds on the following Friday, and would not be back until the Monday, so that there would be no church services next Sunday!

An altogether more pleasant village is Flamstead, which has remained aloof from the A5 and still has a genuine rural air about it despite much modern building. Its crumbling old flint and brick church of St Leonard has a series of poorly preserved but fascinating wall paintings, dating from the thirteenth century, which were only rediscovered in 1930-2. When I went there a group of small boys, at a loose end during the school holidays, greeted me in the porch – where they were sitting to eat their iced lollies – with the information that the door was locked because of vandalism. "Look, it sez 'ere," they said, showing me the notice. "But the front door's open," they added. It was, and I went in to find a lady, aloft on a tower of scaffolding, restoring some of the paintings, faded and indistinct, high up near the oak roof beams in the nave. She was carefully removing grime and wax, a few square inches at a time. She had worked in churches all over England, and told me that the paintings at Flamstead are the best in Hertfordshire except for those in St Albans Abbey.

The church also contains memorials to the Saunders and Sebright families, who owned the manor of Beechwood, to the west, and it was here in May 1808 that John Gully beat Bob Gregson in a fight of twenty-seven rounds that lasted an hour and a quarter. Prizefighting was illegal at the time, but Sir John Sebright, who promoted it to revive his failing fortune, was a magistrate and so, it seems, no questions were asked, and the fight attracted an enormous crowd. Gully subsequently became a race-horse owner, winning the Derby in 1832, and then was M.P. for Pontefract.

Markyate used to be stretched along Watling Street, and indeed still is, but the modern A5 bypasses it so that the children of the village can cross the street in comparative safety, unlike Redbourn. The village has been known in the past as Market Street and Markyate Street, but the more obvious name is incorrect, and Markyate, we are told, means "the gate at the boundary". The oldest inn in the village is The Sun, originally built in the sixteenth century, and it is said to have been a favourite resort of highwaymen. There is a story that Dick Turpin spent a night there once and stole the landlord's horse when he left next morning. Watling Street was certainly a profitable area of operation for highwaymen. In 1697 the county's chief constable reported that the roads were "so infested with robbers that it is highly dangerous for persons to travel with any sums of money". But Dick Turpin is a close rival of Nell Gwynne in Hertfordshire folklore for the dubious distinction of having slept in the most beds, and Markyate has a much more interesting story to tell about a highway robber who actually lived there.

Across the A5 from the village, surrounded by a brick wall, are the grounds of a house called Markyate Cell. The village church is tucked into a corner of these grounds, reached beyond a stately row of lime trees (not an avenue of elms, as Pevsner states). The house stands on the site of a nunnery founded in the twelfth century. At the dissolution of the monasteries, one Humphrey Bourchier built a mansion there, and Edward VI subsequently granted the estate to George Ferrers of St Albans, whose family lived there until the seventeenth century. The last of the Ferrers at Markyate married a very young girl named Katherine, and soon left her a widow, and it is said that she then, although a noblewoman, became a highway robber, dressing as a man and leaving her room at night via a passage which led to the stables. The servants were mystified by their repeated discoveries in the mornings of a tired horse covered with foam.

At length, however, Lady Ferrers, only twenty-five years old, was shot by one of her intended victims, and managing to get back to the house, fell dead at the door of her room. Soon there were stories that her ghost had been seen, riding a coal black horse on Watling Street, or walking in the grounds of the house. About this time the place was owned by Thomas Coppin, who endowed the school at Markyate in which William Cowper suffered so much bullying. Then in 1825 the estate was bought by Daniel Goodson Adye, a J.P. and Deputy-Lieutenant of the county, and he set about rebuilding the mansion on a smaller scale. But when he tried to open the doorway where Lady Ferrers had been found dead, and which had been sealed up for 150 years, no local workman could be induced to do the job, and Mr Adye had to pay men to come up from London and open the room, which was full of bats.

Cussans says that the story "in this present year of 1878 is religiously believed in by the majority of the inhabitants of Markyate Street". A popular film called *The Wicked Lady* was based on the story in the 'fifties, starring Margaret Lockwood and James Mason. How much of the legend is true we shall probably never know, but it is a good story, and an appropriate one with which to leave this ancient and eventful route.

If you come up this way on the train from London, there is a brief view of St Albans, as you pass the old Handley Page airfield, which is like a seventeenth-century Dutch landscape – the cathedral tower rising from a wide flat panorama beneath a huge sky. By the time you pass the Verulam Golf Course, only seconds later, the impression has already gone, and the scene becomes all too English. The city lies before you, and as you emerge from the railway station into Victoria Street, it does not appear a very promising prospect.

IV

THE CITY OF MARTYRS

St Albans, although neither the administrative capital of Hertfordshire nor its largest town, has exercised the most powerful influence on the development of the county during the long centuries since the Romans came to Britain. What is more, it has been one of the most highly privileged towns in England. In pre-Christian times it was a "prehistoric metropolis" (to use Sir Mortimer Wheeler's words). The Romans probably made it a 'municipium', according its people Roman citizenship, and in medieval times it was a 'Liberty' ruled by the Abbot and not by the King. Even after the dissolution of the monasteries St Albans retained this unique position, being governed by a common council, and it was only in 1877, when the borough became a cathedral city, that it lost most of these self-governing privileges, exchanging secular independence for ecclesiastical status.

Until the sixteenth century, the history of St Albans was, in very broad terms, the history of Hertfordshire, and we must therefore return to the story we left in the first chapter with the defeat of Cassivelaunus by Julius Caesar. The routed Catuvellauni set up their new headquarters at Prae Wood, to the west of the present St Albans, on ground rising above the River Ver. Evidence of metalwork, pottery and the minting of coins has been found there, and it is clear from the coins that the first Verulamium was pre-Roman. It did not remain the tribal capital for long, however, this having moved to Colchester by about AD 40 under Cunobelinus – Shakespeare's Cymbeline.

In AD 43, when the Emperor Claudius ordered a fresh invasion of Britain under Aulus Plautius, the first Roman Verulamium began to rise beside the river and the new military road which we know as Watling Street, and the local inhabitants were absorbed by the city and themselves absorbed Roman culture and civilization. No doubt the city was built by local labour under Roman supervision, and it was certainly planned with Roman precision, having an orderly street layout with a drainage system, and single storey houses of timber frames and wattle-and-daub walls; the whole city was surrounded by protective earthworks. But it was not a military garrison for the Roman legions, who were not required to linger where they had already come to terms with the native population.

Whilst the army of occupation was moving northwards, however, the Iceni of East Anglia, less ready to submit to Rome than their neighbours, raised a revolt under Boudicca, the widow of their late king. She had been scourged by the Romans and her daughters raped, and with the savagery of a wounded tiger she led her people on the garrison at Colchester in AD 61, and then on to Verulamium. Both towns were destroyed by fire and indiscriminate slaughter, and those taken captive were butchered with sickening cruelty. Meanwhile, the Roman governor, Suetonius Paulinus, had had time to recall troops to the area and prepare a counter-attack as the Iceni descended on London, and Imperial military efficiency crushed the revolt and avenged the slaughter which Verulamium had suffered, Boudicca apparently choosing to commit suicide rather than be taken by the Romans. According to Tacitus, 150,000 people were killed in Boudicca's raids and the Roman reprisals, and though this figure is now considered to be an exaggeration, the massacre was clearly of appalling dimensions.

A new Verulamium then began to grow on the ashes of the old. By AD 79 it had been rebuilt on a larger scale, and during the next hundred years it developed - untroubled by strife - into an important city, surrounded by walls of flint and brick, traversed by Watling Street, and having temples, public offices, a forum and a theatre. The forum was on the site of the present St Michael's churchyard, and the theatre - the only Roman theatre to be seen in Britain - is a few yards down the course of the original Watling Street.

It was built between AD 125 and 150 and was constructed on the Greek model - semi-circular in shape - with seating for about 1,500 people.

Serious professional excavation of Verulamium began in 1930 under the direction of Mortimer Wheeler. Miss Kathleen Kenyon excavated the theatre, and later work was carried out by Dr Sheppard Frere. One of the early discoveries was the skeleton of a middle-aged Belgic woman who was found to have suffered from rheumatoid arthritis. An altogether more pleasing find was the bronze figurine of Venus, eight inches high, which can be seen in the Verulamium Museum.* Although the chief deities of the Verulamium temples are not known, the presence here of the goddess of love and fertility, dating - in this case - from the second century AD, is appropriate. Caesar promoted her worship, as he claimed descent from her. The almost-naked goddess extends her hands in a life-embracing gesture, and though she was soon to be denounced by the Christians, her irrepressible spirit and significance have survived to this day.

Although the rebuilt Verulamium was the administrative centre of a territory at peace, and not a military station, any signs of disturbance in the *status quo* were ruthlessly suppressed by the ruling powers, and at some point in the city's history - generally assumed, without much evidence, to have been during the persecution of Christians by the Emperor Diocletian - a Roman soldier named Albanus was executed for protecting a priest who had converted him. To the Romans it was (like the execution of a Jewish rabble-rouser in Palestine during the reign of Tiberius) no more than a routine incident in local government, but it assumed a significance for the local Christians which had great consequences for Verulamium and for Hertfordshire. For it seems that some time afterwards they built a shrine on the site of the soldier's martyrdom, across the river on the hill outside the city walls.

When the Rescript of the Emperor Honorius in 410 recalled what remained of the occupying army to shore up the crumbling edifice of the empire in Rome itself, it left Britain, as Gibbon put it, "abandoned, without defence, to the

*The statuette has been stolen twice. It was returned after the first theft, but at the time of writing is still missing after the second.

Saxon pirates and the savages of Ireland and Caledonia". Left to its own devices, and independent for the first time in 350 years, Verulamium began to decay as the people gradually moved across the river and a new town grew up round the shrine of the Christian martyr. The bricks and stones of the Roman city were taken to build new houses, new streets and new shops, and the theatre became a rubbish dump – a sure sign of descent into the Dark Ages. Then Saxon invasions ended the long period of peace, and the disintegration of Verulamium was accelerated. The town that developed under Saxon domination beside it was called Watlingcaester, and here in 793, so the old chroniclers tell us, Offa, the King of Mercia, founded a Benedictine Abbey where the shrine of Albanus had stood.

During the next 250 years, the monastery gained increasing power over the surrounding areas, whilst St Alban's town grew up around it. The sixth abbot, Ulsinus, was the founder of the modern city. He gave the land on which the town was built, and founded the three churches at its gates – St Peter's, St Stephen's and St Michael's. Two rows of houses lined the wide triangular street that was to become the market place, the abbey standing at the widest end. Ulsinus is also credited, usually, with the foundation of St Albans School, but there is no evidence for this, although the school is certainly one of the oldest in the country – older than Eton and Winchester.

The achievements of Ulsinus apart, however, it has to be said that no scriptwriter for Monty Python's Flying Circus, nor specialist in West End farce, could have dreamed up a more ludicrous scenario than the one solemnly presented by the historians of the Saxon abbots. That veneration of relics which was an obsessive feature of the early Christian Church was responsible for a long-drawn-out wrangle in St Albans monastery over a pile of rotting bones supposed to be those of Albanus the martyr.

When the Danes were making their raids on the Saxon kingdom in the ninth and tenth centuries, they claimed that they had stolen the bones and taken them to Odense (where the cathedral is still dedicated to St Alban). The abbot of the time, however, sent two monks to Denmark in disguise to try to recover the bones, which they claimed to have done, despite Danish assertions that these were not the genuine bones. Then, when further Danish raids were anticipated, the bones were deposited for safe keeping in the monastery at Ely, but after they had supposedly been returned to St Albans, the monks at Ely claimed they still had the genuine bones there, and St Albans had fakes. The abbot of St Albans then retorted that he had never sent the genuine bones to Ely in the first place, having hidden them in a wall and sent bogus bones to Ely. It was none other than Pope Adrian IV who brought this protracted dispute to an end in favour of – guess who – St Albans. But as the bones in question were unlikely to have been those of Albanus in the first place, probably neither St Albans nor Ely nor Odense ever had the gruesome relics that each laid passionate claim to.

It was after the Norman Conquest when St Albans rose to its position of pre-eminence among the abbeys of England. Archbishop Lanfranc had Paul de Caen, who is believed to have been his son, appointed Abbot of St Albans in 1077, and he set about rebuilding the abbey. The Saxon monastery buildings were demolished almost without trace, only the bakehouse and buttery being left intact, and within about eleven years a great new Norman church had been more or less completed, although it was not rededicated until 1116. Since the only local building stone was flint, the new Christian abbey was built, ironically, with Roman brick brought in cartloads from the ruined pagan city across the river.

By the thirteenth century, the abbey of St Alban had become one of the richest and most powerful religious establishments in England, and was renowned as the country's greatest centre of learning and historical composition.* Roger of Wendover and Matthew Paris are the most famous of the abbey's historians. It had a great library, a guest hall for reception of the many important visitors who came, and stabling for 300 horses. As well as its huge area of land in Hertfordshire, it had property in Buckinghamshire and Bed-

*The *Anglo-Saxon Chronicle* records that in 1124 the Abbot of St Albans accompanied the Archbishops of Canterbury and York on a visit to Rome, where they were received with great ceremony by Pope Honorius.

fordshire, Norfolk and Northumberland, and the town, itself the property of the abbey, had won exemption from being answerable to the King.

St Albans was partly surrounded by a ditch, possibly with a wall on its inner side. The ditch – which became known as the Tonman Ditch – can still be seen in places – notably the stretch running from the Ancient Briton inn to Porters Wood and now called Beech Bottom Dyke. This particular section is in a direct line with the ditch called The Slad at Wheathampstead, and was proved by Wheeler to be Belgic in origin, not medieval. South-east of the abbey, near the river, was the Sopwell Priory, converted into a private mansion after the dissolution, and Boleyn Drive, near the ruins, recalls the unsubstantiated rumour that Henry VIII married his second wife there.

In the fourteenth century came that disaster which can be seen, with hindsight, as the beginning of the end of the abbey's domination of so much of Hertfordshire, though the end was still 200 years away. The Black Death killed at least half the abbey's monks, as well as the Abbot himself, Michael de Mentmore, who died on Easter Day 1349. Probably the monks invited death by their self-sacrificing attendance on stricken townsfolk. There is evidence to suggest that, terrible as the plague unquestionably was, its effects in Hertfordshire were less serious than in some other counties. The wealthy and efficiently run manors of the abbey were quickly reorganized and agriculture continued unhindered by the great changes that were brought about elsewhere by the scarcity of man-power. But such a massive calamity was bound to have long-term effects, and combined with bad harvests and the inevitable corruption resulting from such power as the abbey had, it led to the involvement of St Albans in the Peasants' Revolt, then the Wars of the Roses, and finally the dissolution of the abbey, which maintained a feudal stranglehold on the populace when, elsewhere, peasants subject to the secular authority were gaining some freedom and self-respect.

The authority of the Abbot had already been challenged before the Black Death came. One of his laws had established a monopoly for his fulling and grinding mills, but offended tradesmen in the town gave work to other millers who offered their services more cheaply. They were not allowed to get away with this show of independence, however, and some were imprisoned, while the Abbot took advantage of his victory by enclosing areas of common land. Further riots occurred at intervals, and the situation came to a head in 1381 under the leadership of a local agitator, William Grindcobbe. Disturbances spread to abbey lands at Watford and Rickmansworth, Berkhamsted and Tring, Redbourn and Sandridge, Codicote and Walden. At St Albans, Grindcobbe, having talked in London with Wat Tyler, who had promised to send 20,000 men to "shave the monks' beards" if the abbot resisted, announced to an exultant gathering in the market-place that they were henceforth free men. But their joy was short-lived. News came from London that Wat Tyler was dead and his armies scattered. At length, the King's army entered the town to crush the rebellion.

The famous rebel preacher John Ball was brought to the town from Hertford Gaol, and a show trial was staged at the Moot Hall. Ball was the first English socialist. He has been called "the embodiment of a people's aspirations", and if Wat Tyler's name is more famous as the active leader of the Peasants' Revolt, Ball was its prophet. After much intimidation of juries, the rebel leaders were condemned to death. Ball, Grindcobbe and thirteen others were hanged, and Ball drawn and quartered, their bodies being hung in chains on gibbets, while the words of the fourteen-year-old King, who was hunting at Ashridge, resounded in the ears of the appalled onlookers: "Serfs you were, and serfs you will remain." The damage was done, however, and thenceforth the authority of the Abbot was in decline.

In 1402 the town built its Clock Tower, a rare surviving example of a town belfry, behind the Eleanor Cross erected to commemorate the passage through the town of the corpse of Eleanor of Castile on its way to London. The bell in the tower was at one time rung at some unearthly hour of the morning to summon apprentices to their work, and after the demolition of the Eleanor Cross, a shop was built on to the tower, as can be seen in old engravings. There was a bull-ring near the market place for the entertainment of the mob.

Eventually the abbey acquired a royal tomb of its own. Humphrey, Duke of Gloucester, was a friend of Abbot John of Wheathampstead, and made grants of land to the monastery. When he died in 1447, he was buried here and still lies in a vault beneath the tomb. Defoe, writing in 1724, has a nice piece about it:

> In this church as some workmen were digging for the repairs of the church, they found some steps which led to a door in a very thick stone wall, which being opened, there was discovered an arched stone vault, and in the middle of it a large coffin near 7 foot long, which being opened, there was in it the corpse of a man, the flesh not consumed, but discoloured; by the arms and other paintings on the wall, it appeared that this must be the body of Humphry Duke of Gloucester, commonly called the good Duke of Gloucester, one of the sons of Henry IV and brother to King Henry V, and by the most indisputable authority, must have lain buried there 277 years.

Popular Gloucester might have been, but he was avaricious and irresponsible, and it is probably just as well that he did not become king, although his nephew, who did, was hardly any improvement on him.

In 1455 the first battle in the Wars of the Roses took place in St Albans. Henry VI and the redoubtable Margaret of Anjou spent the night before the battle at Hall Place, and held a council of war next morning in the Moot Hall – the building now occupied by W. H. Smith & Son. The King had 2,000 men in St Albans that day, but he was recovering from a long period of insanity and was probably oblivious of the significance of the proceedings, Margaret undoubtedly being the effective ruler and commander-in-chief. The Yorkists attacked this army in St Peter's Street, wounded the King and took him prisoner. The Abbot, still John of Wheathampstead, saw the fighting and recorded that: "Here you saw one fall with his brains dashed out, there another with a broken arm, a third with a cut throat, and a fourth with a pierced chest, and the whole street was full of dead corpses."

Though the English population at large remained generally indifferent to, and in the short term unaffected by, the quarrels between the houses of York and Lancaster, blood flowed twice in the streets of St Albans. Six years after the battle in St Peter's Street, Bernard's Heath, north of the town centre, was the scene of another encounter, when the positions were reversed. Margaret's army advanced on the Yorkists who held the town, inflicted a heavy defeat on them and rescued the King, who was found under an oak tree, laughing at the goings-on. Who, one is inclined to ask, was the insane one here? Margaret wreaked vengeance on the Yorkists and on St Albans by letting her troops loot and ravage the town at will. The battle is significant in military history for the first use of small firearms in England.

Printing has long been one of the principal trades in St Albans, and its origins are usually traced back to about 1480, four years after Caxton set up his press at Westminster. A volume called *The Boke of Saynt Albans* was printed in 1486, said to be by Juliana Berners, a prioress at the Sopwell Nunnery. The printer was referred to as "one sometyme scholemayster of Saynt Alban" who printed six books in Latin and two in English. Unfortunately, however, there is no trace of such a lady at Sopwell, nor of the nameless schoolmaster, and it has been plausibly suggested that this press may have been at Westminster too, part of which was known as "Little St Albans" at the time.

In 1521 Thomas Wolsey was ominously appointed Abbot of St Albans, but the tyranny of the abbey over the town's population had ended with the Peasants' Revolt and subsequent events. Wolsey never resided in the town, and by the time of his death the writing was on the wall for the abbey and its monks, reduced to thirty-eight by then. Nine years later the abbey and all the monastery buildings and its widespread property were surrendered to the King. All the buildings except the abbey church, the gatehouse and the stables were subsequently demolished. Much of the local property was acquired by Sir Richard Lee, who built himself a house on the site of the Sopwell Priory, and when the town was granted its first charter by Edward VI, constituting it a free borough "corporate in deed, fact and name for ever", the townsfolk bought the abbey from the Crown for use as their parish church. The domination of much of Hertfordshire by the abbot and monks of St Albans, in decline for so long, had finally ended, but lest the natives of the town should forget the authority of the church, Bishop Bonner, that zealous henchman of Bloody Mary, had a Protestant baker from Barnet, George Tankerfield, burnt at the stake near the abbey in 1555, to impress the natives who, it was alleged, had no martyr-spirit!

Thenceforth, St Albans became a relatively quiet and uneventful market town, notable chiefly for its school, by this time styled Grammar School, which was carried on in the Lady Chapel of the abbey until 1871, and then in the Great Gatehouse until its present buildings were erected early in this century. The schoolboys of the seventeenth century had no Unidentified Flying Objects to exercise their minds on. Life was a matter of certainties then, not doubts, and if something airborne was spotted it could only be Mother Haggy, the most famous St Albans witch, off somewhere on her broomstick. She could turn herself into a lion, a hare or a cat, and must have been a lot more canny than another St Albans witch who was ducked in the river to test her guilt or innocence. Unable to sink, even though she thrust her head below the surface, she came out and crowned her guilt by admitting that one of her imps had leapt upon her breast under the water.

Not that such rituals and primitive beliefs ended with the disappearance of the witch-craze, even in St Albans. In 1899, at the prison in Grimston Road which later became a council depot, a 22-year-old girl named Mary Ansell was hanged for a murder she probably did not commit, and even if she did commit it, she was clearly insane and should not have been hanged. But the dice were loaded against her. She was supposed to have sent a poisoned cake to her sister in Leavesden Asylum, so that she could collect the insurance money, and as an elderly resident of the town who remembered the case told the *Herts Advertiser* a few years ago: "We all felt she must be guilty as they were hanging her." Mary Ansell was a martyr to that barbaric belief that justice resides in vengeance. Hopefully she was the last in a long line of sacrificial victims that started sixteen or more hundred years earlier with a soldier named Albanus, and included John Ball and William Grindcobbe, George Tankerfield and all the unnamed witches and dissenters who died because their beliefs did not coincide with those of the people set in authority over them.

Apart from Sir Francis Bacon of Gorhambury, the most distinguished resident of St Albans was Sarah Jennings, the Duchess of Marlborough. She was born at Sandridge in 1660, and when she married John Churchill she received Holywell House, at the foot of Holywell Hill, as part of her dowry. She and her husband spent much time there, and Queen Anne and George I visited the house. As High Steward of St Albans, Marlborough succeeded Sir Harbottle Grimston, who bought Gorhambury and became Speaker of the House of Commons under Charles II. As Marlborough rose in rank and status, his wife rose in her imperious domination of the court through her influence on her childhood friend Anne, and when the Queen finally got rid of the Duchess, the disgrace of the Duke soon followed. His corruption and duplicity were known, and collaboration with the enemy suspected. After Marlborough's death the Dowager Duchess, known in her younger days as a court beauty and called "La Belle Jennings", was commonly nicknamed "Viceroy Sarah" and "Her Graceless". Horace Walpole says she used to turn her head away when offering the Queen her gloves or fan, "as if the Queen had offensive smells". Old and infirm, Sarah made enemies of everyone. One personal vendetta led her to hang in her sitting-room a portrait of Lady Anne Egerton, of Ashridge, on which Sarah had blackened the face and written underneath "She is blacker within."

Although the Duchess had not been wealthy when she married Churchill, she was, like Benjamin Styles of Moor Park, among the few who made a fortune out of the South Sea Bubble, which left so many ruined men when it burst, and she built and endowed the large and simply styled Marlborough Almshouses in Hatfield Road. She had a statue of Queen Anne made for the courtyard, but it was never set there, and is now at Blenheim Palace.

St Albans was an important coaching station on the London–Holyhead route, but its roads were in an appalling condition. At the end of the eighteenth century Telford cut the new London Road to divert traffic from the dangerous winding route through Sopwell Lane, Holywell Hill, High Street, George Street and Fishpool Street to the line of the original Roman road, and this led to the decline and fall of the old coaching inns that lined the east side of Holywell Hill. Only the White Hart remains, and that much restored, but it was here where Hogarth made his studies of Lord Lovat, on his way to execution at Tower Hill, and here also where, in 1761, the town demonstrated its independence by the extraordinary gesture of declaring war on Spain three weeks before the national government did so!

The new road soon had stories to tell as hair-raising as those of the old. In 1819, a fatal collision occurred between the Chester Mail and the Holyhead Mail, and the drivers, George Butler and Thomas Perdy, were indicted for the wilful murder of a Holyhead passenger. The coaches had started to race at Highgate and crashed into each other when galloping into St Albans at eleven o'clock at night. It was advanced as a defence by the Post Office that the Holyhead Mail ought to have been at Redbourn a quarter of an hour before the other. Alas, that such conscientiousness is no more! The two men were, nevertheless, convicted of manslaughter and spent eighteen months in prison. A few years later, at almost the same spot, where the railway bridge now crosses London Road, a coach came upon another nearly buried in a huge snowdrift during one of the worst snowstorms on record. Two ladies were inside it, and said that the postboy had left two hours before to get help!

As late as the middle of last century, at least one baker in St Albans was claiming to make hot-cross buns for Good Friday to a recipe for which the abbey had become famous among the townsfolk. Said to have been first made by Father Rocliff in 1361, the recipe had been a jealously guarded secret of the abbey until the dissolution, and it is hardly surprising that local bakers tried to cash in on the fame of the buns, whether they really knew the recipe or not.

Meanwhile, the abbey was falling into a shocking state of disrepair. Celia Fiennes, the indefatigable seventeenth-century traveller, wrote that "the whole Church is so worn away that it mourns for some charitable person to help repaire it". No such charitable person appeared, however, until nearly 200 years later, by which time the nave was practically a ruin. Some repairs were carried out by Sir Gilbert Scott from 1860 onwards with money raised by public subscription, but the abbey was large and the population of St Albans small, and a committee formed to organize restoration of this enormous parish church found itself helpless because of lack of funds. And in 1878, Scott died. It was then that the great ogre of St Albans Abbey appeared on the scene.

Sir Edmund Beckett was a ruthless, overbearing and cantankerous member of a Yorkshire family - a professional lawyer and an amateur architect and clock-maker, and inheritor of a fortune made from the railway boom - who came to St Albans and presented himself to the Restoration Committee as their saviour. He was known as the designer of the Westminster clock popularly and wrongly called Big Ben. He would restore the abbey entirely at his own expense and to his own design.

Whatever the committee thought of this Queen's Counsel's arguments, his money was most eloquent. Besides, Queen Victoria had granted the town a charter, making it a city. (By an absurd grammatical error it became the City of St Albans rather than of St Alban.) The abbey church was now a cathedral. It *must* be restored to a dignity becoming its new status. In 1880, Beckett was granted a faculty by the new Bishop which gave him virtually a free hand in restoring the church. It was not long before Beckett, who became Lord Grimthorpe during his work on the abbey, was in dispute with the members of the committee, who included Earl

Cowper, Sir John Evans, and Mr John Toulmin of Childwickbury. The last, who as Secretary of the Restoration Committee had suddenly got cold feet over the Grimthorpe *carte blanche* and wrote to *The Times* about it, came in for a typical Grimthorpe lambasting in the Press, where his lordship was wont to air his often offensive and occasionally libellous opinions on the iniquities of doctors and professional architects, among others. Toulmin, said Grimthorpe, had made "a little mistake of £1600 in the accounts", and if he sent off his dirty linen "to be washed with the sheets of The Times", Grimthorpe would have no objection to "mangle it for him".

Sir Nikolaus Pevsner is curiously reticent in criticizing what Grimthorpe did at St Albans, on the grounds that if it had not been for his generosity, there would probably be no abbey left at all. But money and good taste have little in common, and I do not see that a man's cash should purchase respect for his vulgar acts and opinions. The wise philanthropist leaves aesthetics to others. Modesty was not one of Lord Grimthorpe's virtues, however. He was a blunt northern industrialist whose reputation preceded him to St Albans, and much of the blame for what he did to the abbey must therefore rest with the committee which allowed him to ride roughshod over them for the sake of his 'brass'. A millionaire who was essentially a mechanical engineer and whose taste in food stopped at boiled beef and fruit tart ought not to have been entrusted with any valuable work of art.

What Grimthorpe actually did was to pull down the west front and rebuild it – with yellow stone – in Victorian Gothic, with an image of himself as St Matthew in the porch, though he professed to deplore idols. He put a circular window in the north transept which has been well described as "a diagram of ball-bearings in the hub of a wheel". He forced vulgarity into an unhappy marriage with austerity, and upon restraint he pressed the spectacular. Preserving the historical character of old buildings he regarded as "modern cant", and when a luncheon was held at the Peahen Hotel to celebrate the opening of the restored nave, someone expressed the opinion that, now that he had done his good work, "the sooner he was called to his heavenly reward the better". But alas, Lord Grimthorpe was to live long enough to bestow his goodness on St Peter's and St Michael's in like manner, rebuilding the tower of the latter church although one of the workmen remarked that if the old one had been left alone it would have stood for ever. One can only gasp at the staggering foolhardiness of St Albans in allowing him to touch it after his work on the abbey and St Peter's, and thank Providence for taking him away before he had a go at St Stephen's.

Even with its architectural crudities, of course, St Albans Abbey (no native calls it the cathedral) remains one of Hertfordshire's greatest buildings. It is the oldest surviving monastic church in Western Europe, and its nave is the longest in the world. Its exterior is best seen from a distance, where its massive Norman tower of Roman brick speaks of its antiquity, but I always find the approach from the Waxhouse Gate (where candles were sold to pilgrims) particularly impressive, despite the Grimthorpe window, and its interior, despite the confusion of styles, still has many delights, not least of which are the thirteenth-century wall paintings which, Pevsner says, are "unique amongst the major churches of England". As I write, some controversy surrounds a plan to build a visitors' centre at the abbey, and I must say it seems to me that both the abbey and the town would profit more by providing somewhere for visitors to park their cars when they arrive.

A few corners of the old town retain enough of their former style and charm to hint at what it was like once – French Row (so called because French soldiers were quartered there in 1217; it had previously been Cordwainers' Row); the long and newly fashionable Fishpool Street, winding towards St Michael's; the backs of the old buildings such as the White Hart; the narrow passages such as Boot Alley and Pudding Lane.

The town's growth has fortunately been mainly to the north, south and east, Marshalswick and St Julians now being among the favoured residential areas, with the result that the cathedral area has been left alone in the triangle formed by the

River Ver and the stylish George Street (once called Cook's Row), and lower Holywell Hill, both lined with timbered buildings and antique shops. On the south side of the abbey, past the Fighting Cocks Inn (once claimed to be the oldest inhabited licensed house in England, though actually a monastery building which only became an inn around 1600), Verulamium stretches away, with fragments of Roman walls here and there, beyond a lake in the landscaped area near the river, forming St Albans' most delightful part, where the ugly Victorian scene that met us on leaving the railway station seems much farther distant than it actually is. For the nine-teenth-century extension of the town, speaking its dates in the names of its streets - Inkerman Road, Alma Road - is no more than a stone's throw from the centre of the city whose new Civic Centre is pleasantly flanked by the Waterend
Barn that was brought here from Sandridge, and an old garden behind a council office in St Peter's Street.

Yet the council's City Hall is less comfortable and agreeable, though larger and more expensive, than the Abbey Theatre, opened in the same year by the amateur Company of Ten in a local tradition of 'do-it-yourself' enterprise that began sixty years earlier with the opening of the Picture Palace, with a proscenium decorated by Fred Karno, on the site of the present Odeon cinema. Built by the pioneer Arthur Melbourne-Cooper, who was born here, it was probably the first purpose-built cinema in the country.

The town seems to have a curious partiality for organ music. As well as its ecclesiastical sponsorship of the biennial Organ Festival, it sounds a more secular note in the Organ Museum founded in 1961 to house a fine collection of fairground and dance organs begun by a retired builder, Charles Hart, after the Second World War. It is a private collection, but is opened to the public on Sunday afternoons.

St Albans today is a city - small, as cities go - of endless fascination, but with a growing air of dereliction about it, and it is beset by a major traffic problem which no one seems unduly anxious to solve, as well as having a bad reputation among women for its lamentable shopping facilities. When the

M1 motorway was opened, it was anticipated that it would take a lot of the traffic away from what had been described, with wild exaggeration, as the busiest crossroads in the country. It failed to do so, however, and the town centre is certainly, at times, a nightmare for old people wanting to cross the streets, and an infuriating bottleneck for drivers (though less so now than when the eccentric vicar of St Stephen's Church regularly increased the chaos by striding into the middle of the road and banging on the window of a car to demand a lift from some total stranger who happened to be going in the direction of his church!). One almost wishes for a return to the early days of the century, when a hundred worthy citizens of St Albans were members of an organization called The Against Travelling on Sunday Union, and the St Albans and Mid-Herts Hospital magnanimously announced that it was open at all times for accidents, "without any recommendation".

St Albans is among the worst sufferers from Hertfordshire's closeness to London, and short of some major and very expensive scheme to divert traffic away from it, it is difficult to see how further deterioration of this very old city can be avoided. The most ludicrous of signs in the city streets must surely be that which traffic thunders past on the A5 as it nears the city centre, saying: "Hospital – Quiet". The comparative ease of a half-hour train journey from London (packed rush-hour trains in winter; everybody reading one another's newspapers and catching one another's colds; staggeringly overheated compartments but all windows tightly shut!) makes the city a favourite commuter centre and property prices are pushed ever upwards. Poor Victorian terraced houses in the back streets, which would almost qualify as slum property in some towns, change hands for £12,000 here.

In some ways, St Albans is an epitome of the so-called advance of civilization and the state of England at present, in which chaos and stress take the place of style and dignity, and pride precedes the fall. The place seems to have a schizoid personality. Uncertain of its identity in the modern world, indecisive as to whether it wants to present itself as an historic

'Joyride', a lively sculpture in Stevenage New Town centre

St Albans cathedral

Harpenden – growth by evolution

Hatfield House

Welwyn Garden City – birth by special creation

The 'George and Dragon', Codicote

The old church of Ayot St Lawrence

The village post office at Bramfield

St Mary's church, Ashwell, with its elaborate 'spike'

The porch of Hitchin parish church

town or a progressive community, it makes no decisions at all and loses on both counts, criticized by shoppers and traders for not being up to date, on the one hand, and by conservationists for not being sufficiently out of date, on the other. It is as if the city, used to the driving force of a single man, were awaiting another Ulsinus or, worse, another Grimthorpe.

V

THE MODERN WAY

THE A6 IS A modern trunk road, following no ancient track or Roman road, but dating mainly from 1826, when Telford's new Holyhead road was constructed. As far as Hertfordshire is concerned, it is relatively short. It does not pass through the county from end to end, like the other roads we are dealing with (although it did before Barnet was exchanged for Potters Bar), but is linked with the A1 near the village of Ridge, whence it makes a fairly straight track to St Albans, leading to the aforementioned chaotic crossroads and then – somewhat shaky after that experience – wobbles off through Harpenden and leaves the county, south of Luton, on its long trek to Carlisle.

Ridge is the burial place of two men famous for their exploits in foreign parts. We have already noticed the grave of one great Alexander in Hertfordshire, and here we find another – Earl Alexander of Tunis. One of the most brilliant professional soldiers of modern times, the success of his strategy in North Africa during the Second World War, when he succeeded Auchinleck as Commander-in-Chief of the Middle East Forces, is regarded as the highlight of the Field Marshal's career, although his management of the Dunkirk evacuation, and his later command of allied forces in Italy, were hardly less brilliant. A man of rather more modesty than many of the officers who served under him, Alexander's grave in this village churchyard covers the bones of one to whom modern Britain owes a great deal.

There is a memorial inside the church to Sir Henry Pope Blount, who travelled in 1634 to Turkey and Egypt and described his experiences in his book *Voyage to the Levant,* which was popular reading in Stuart England. Sir Henry figures in the *Brief Lives* of John Aubrey, who says that "drunkenness he much exclaimed against, but wenching he allowed". Not only allowed it, in fact, but took the view that it was "far cheaper and safer to lie with common wenches than with ladies of quality"; an opinion for which, as Aubrey tells us, Sir Henry was called to account.

Sir Henry was born at Tyttenhanger (which derives its name, we are assured, from "the wooded slope of Tida"). Be that as it may, Sir Henry Blount is supposed to have been the builder of the brick mansion known as Tyttenhanger Park, which has a staircase carved by Grinling Gibbons. The mansion is on the site of an earlier house which was a country retreat for the Abbot of St Albans, and Henry VIII and Wolsey are said to have stayed in it when the plague was raging in London. At the dissolution it was acquired by Sir Henry Pope Blount's ancestor, Sir Thomas Pope, who was the founder of Trinity College, Oxford, and he gave the manor to the college, but it was reconveyed to him and his heirs on the condition that they annually presented to the college a fat buck and a hogshead of claret.

Tyttenhanger is the site of a lost medieval village. Thirty-one people died there when the Black Death struck, but whether the remaining villagers deserted the place as a result of that, or its destruction was at the hands of the Abbot in order to create pasture land or his country park, we do not know. Hertfordshire's lost villages are still cloaked in mystery compared with those of many another county. This is partly due to the fact that, Hertfordshire having no natural building stone, its medieval houses were wooden, so the telltale uneven fields of the Midlands, with stone foundations just below the surface, do not occur here. Aerial photography during the long, dry summer of 1976 has shown up some interesting traces of buildings, however, and no doubt we shall learn more about medieval Hertfordshire as time goes on.

At Salisbury Hall we are on firmer ground. This house was built by Sir John Cuttes, Henry VIII's Treasurer, on land surrounded by a Norman moat, and at the end of the seventeenth century it was modernized by Sir Jeremiah Snow, who placed above the panelling in the hall eight plaster medallions with the heads of Roman emperors in profile. These are often said to have come from Sopwell Priory in St Albans, but it seems hardly likely that pagan despots would be permitted to gaze down from the walls of a Christian nunnery, quite apart from the fact that the style of the medallions is post-dissolution, so perhaps they came from the house built on the site of the priory *after* the dissolution.

At any rate, Salisbury Hall was visited many times by the Merry Monarch, and it is said that Nell Gwynne stayed in the lodge nearby. Poor Nell! She was nineteen when Charles first sampled her fruits, and dead by the time she was thirty-seven. The illiterate actress may have been saved from starving, after Charles's death, by the new king, James II, but there was no saving her from the tattle of village gossips, and it is a moot point whether Nell Gwynne or Dick Turpin is the most absurdly fictionalized character in Hertfordshire folklore. The story told of Salisbury Hall is that Nell held her first child by the King over the moat and threatened to drop him in unless he was granted a title, whereupon Charles cried: "Nelly, Nelly, don't kill the Duke of St Albans."

Lady Randolph Churchill lived here later and, in the present century, Sir Nigel Gresley, the locomotive engineer. During the 1939-45 war, the prototype of the versatile de Havilland Mosquito aircraft was designed and built here, where it can still be seen when the house is opened to the public.

Salisbury Hall is only a stone's throw from London Colney, through which the River Colne flows, beneath a bridge built in 1772. Cussans was able to describe it as a "picturesque little village", but no one could echo his opinion today, and the record in the parish accounts of a payment of ten shillings at the Swan Inn during 'processioning', in the year after the bridge was built, is difficult to imagine now. It referred to the tradition of 'beating the parish bounds' which was done during Rogation Week. The lord of the manor and various officers of the parish toured the boundaries calling for blessings on the corn crops.

The stained glass windows in the church of St Peter were designed by Ruskin's friend the Marchioness of Waterford, the artistic and unlikely wife of a mad fox-hunting Irish peer. She spent some time at Tyttenhanger with her maternal grandmother, the Countess of Hardwicke, when the church had not been long built.

The A6 skirts London Colney before plunging beneath the railway and into St Albans, then comes out of the city on the north side past the modern inn called The Ancient Briton, where Beech Bottom Dyke begins more or less in line with a Roman road going off towards Sandridge and the Devil's Dyke at Wheathampstead, and then to Colchester.

Sandridge has managed to keep some of its rural character, lying amid fields and country lanes beyond St Albans, but within pleasant walking distance. Its church contains Roman brick, but the tower collapsed in 1688, and the cost of restoration must have contributed to the lengths to which the churchwardens went in 1732, when they forbade the giving of any parish money for foxes, polecats or hedgehogs, and limited the minister's allowance to ten shillings a year. The house of God was one thing, it seems, but his servants and creatures were not worth an increase in the parish rates, dead or alive.

Waterend House, north-east of the village, is where Sarah Jennings is thought to have been born, and when the future Duke of Marlborough was made a peer, he chose the title Lord Churchill of Sandridge as a mark of respect to his wife. The house was built by her father, Sir John Jennings, and one of its fine timbered barns was dismantled in the 1920s and re-erected in St Albans, where it is in service as a restaurant. The family responsible for this enterprise, the Thrales, are also an old-established Sandridge family, and one of them married Hester Lynch Salusbury of Offley, none other than the famous Mrs Thrale well known to readers of Boswell's life of Dr Johnson.

North of the village is No Man's Land Common, which is said to get its name from the fact that it was disputed territory between the abbots of St Albans, who owned Sandridge, and those of Westminster, who owned Wheathampstead. In more recent times it has been the popular scene of horse-racing and prize-fighting, and a sensational fight took place there in 1833 when one 'Deaf' Burke fought Simon Byrne, the Irish champion. The fight went to ninety-nine rounds and lasted three and a quarter hours, ending in victory for Burke. But four days later Byrne died, and 'Deaf' Burke and his seconds were tried for manslaughter at Hertford Assizes. A doctor testified, however, that Byrne's death was not due to the injuries he received in the fight, so the defendants were acquitted.

The large and interesting church of St Helen at Wheathampstead contains many memorials to the Garrard family, one of whom, Elizabeth, though she was not married till the "39th yeare of her age", in 1632, gave birth to fourteen children. One of the descendants of this Elizabethan progeny, and the last to own the old family home at Lamer House, which stood in its own park near Gustard Wood, was Apsley Cherry-Garrard, the author of *The Worst Journey in the World.*

Cherry-Garrard was one of the youngest members of Captain Scott's second expedition to Antarctica. He was taken as assistant zoologist to Dr Edward Wilson, and was seriously considered by Scott as a possible member of the small party which was to make the journey to the South Pole, but having concluded that the older men withstood the cold better than the young, Scott took Oates instead, Cherry-Garrard having already been exposed, during a scientific expedition with Wilson and Bowers earlier, to the lowest temperatures then recorded on the Antarctic continent. Cherry-Garrard was one of those who found the bodies of Scott, Wilson and Bowers in their last camp on the return from the Pole, and it was he who suggested the words from Tennyson which were carved on the cross they left there: "To strive, to seek, to find, and not to yield."

The Bull Inn at Wheathampstead is well known. A modernized timbered building dating from the seventeenth century, it was once a post office, but as The Bull in later days it was frequented by, among others, the great actor Sir Herbert Beerbohm Tree. Although the village no longer has a railway line running through it, Wheathampstead has a surprising air of industry about it, for right at its centre is the works of the Murphy Chemical Company, which specializes in the production of horticultural chemicals.

Wheathampstead was called 'Watamestede' after the Norman Conquest. But before we take this as evidence for that hypothetical Saxon nobleman we encountered at Watford, let us bear in mind the case of Harpenden which, like Wheathampstead, was for centuries owned by the abbots of Westminster.

"Harpenden," states Sir Henry Chauncy boldly, "is situated upon an Hill, from whence it derives its name." Now this sentence tells us two things at once. First, that Sir Henry Chauncy never *went* to Harpenden, and second, that we should be cautious in jumping to conclusions about the meanings of place-names. For over the past centuries the name has been spelt Harpendena and Herpendene; and as the town, so far from being upon a hill, actually lies in a valley, it is clear that the ending comes not from the Celtic 'dun' (a hill) but from 'dene' (a hollow).

Harpenden was once described as one of Hertfordshire's prettiest villages, and indeed, its layout has all the ingredients that usually go to make a typical English village so attractive. Its church is tucked away at a quiet corner of the village green, and its tree-lined main street, with a number of old inns along its length, opens out on to a large common. In the middle of the last century, it had a population of 2,500.

At about that time, however, the licensee of the Cross Keys, one Henry Oldaker, established an annual horse-race on Harpenden Common, which continued until the beginning of the First World War, and Cussans deplored the fact that ". . . for two days in the year all the London pick-pockets, sharpers and blackguards who happen to be out of gaol, are permitted to make Harpenden their own, and to make travelling in a first-class carriage of the Midland Railway a danger to men, and an impossibility to ladies".

Perhaps Cussans was a little hard on the event. We get a different view of it from Lady Mary Carbery, who visited the races as a child with her family, the Toulmins of Childwickbury, and describes their maids having their fortunes told by a gypsy, while a policeman looked the other way, and a cheap-jack doctor in a top hat and black coat "shouting from a cart about his mirryaculous cure-all 'ealth pills".

> Before long a pack of Childwick people sidle up, the mothers in braided stuff dresses and wearing their 'lahstick-sides' (Sunday boots). "Look-a-ther," a woman says, "see our liddle misses a-settin up in their noo 'ats a-lookin' like Mornin' Glories." We wave, and Papa takes them to a tent, and orders them sandwiches and beer.

The races, in any case, were only held for two days in May each year, but the railway, which opened in 1868, was permanent, and so was the exploding population of business executives of London, St Albans and Luton, for whom were built the "hundreds of phoney half-timbered residences" which Pevsner found so distasteful. Nevertheless, Arthur Mee thought Harpenden "a country town of great delight" with an air "as sweet and pure as any corner of the British Isles", and even when I first saw it, much later, I thought it a place of great charm.

Alas, no longer. Its streets have now been awarded yellow lines – those medal ribbons presented in the campaign against pollution; dubious battle honours, to say the least, which are themselves – to change the metaphor – a part of the disease they are meant to cure.

The name of Harpenden has been bandied about in all the corners of Britain in recent years, via television, for the town's best-known resident is a certain Mr Bartholomew, better known as Eric Morecambe. Another famous show-business resident of Harpenden was the actress Ellen Terry, who lived here for seven years with the architect Edward Godwin in a house he had built at Fallows Green, and she gave birth there to their children Edward and Edith Craig.

On the south-western outskirts of Harpenden lies the Rothamsted Experimental Station, which sounds like some modern laboratory of nuclear physics or radio astronomy, but is in fact something more prosaic and infinitely more vital – the home of the Lawes Agricultural Trust. John Bennet Lawes, who was born here, came into the estate which had been the property of his ancestors since the seventeenth century. He devoted himself to running the farm, and thus began his lifelong interest in soils and plant nutrition and pathology. Eventually he was joined in this valuable work by Sir Joseph Gilbert, and the two men created the world's first agricultural science laboratory. Sir John Lawes died in 1900, a much-honoured man, and there is a memorial to him in Harpenden church. His great work continues at Rothamsted under the Trust he set up with an endowment of £100,000, and this little-known benefactor of mankind, an amiable sportsman who once caught a 54-pound salmon which stood for a long time in the records as the largest ever landed with a fly, was responsible for research which has helped to increase the world's food supply. During the 1939–45 war, Rothamsted was host to the evacuated department of Professor J. B. S. Haldane, whose scientific work for the Admiralty, sometimes carried out at considerable risk to his own life, helped development of submarine escape methods, and made possible such underwater exploits as the attack by one-man submarines on the German battleship *Tirpitz*.

Beyond the Batford end of Harpenden, over the River Lea, we come across Charles Lamb for the first time, for the farm at Mackerye End is the subject of his well-known essay "Mackery End in Hertfordshire". John of Wheathampstead, the Abbot of St Albans, was born in an older house on the site of the fine seventeenth-century mansion with Dutch-style gables which can still be seen there, but it is the farm to the south that Lamb was concerned with, for he spent much time there as a child with his great-aunt, Ann Gladman, who was housekeeper to Thomas Hawkins at the mansion. Hawkins was related to the Garrards already mentioned.

"The oldest thing I remember," Lamb wrote over forty years later, "is Mackery End; or Mackerel End, as it is spelt, perhaps more properly, in some old maps of Hertfordshire; a farm-house, – delightfully situated within a gentle walk from

Wheathampstead." He would have walked through Harpenden and the stylish Hatching Green on his way to Redbourn, where lived his friend Thomas Manning, who became the first Englishman to visit the Dalai Lama in Tibet.

Although the A6 leaves Hertfordshire as it goes beyond Harpenden, the county boundary runs more or less parallel with it for some way beyond Luton, and some of the villages near this part of the border belong to this chapter, for though they are *in* the county, they are not strictly *of* it, being peopled largely by the business personnel of Luton and London.

Kimpton and Whitwell are of little significance in the story of the county, but some of their old customs are recorded, and bring a touch of country tradition to this chapter of town houses and famous people. So do some of the names in the district, such as Claggybottom, Barleybeans and Cuckoldscross. Palm Sunday was known as Fig Sunday in these and other villages, when it was the custom, if the weather was fine, to 'keep worsel' – making merry with family and friends out of doors and eating dessert figs, or making puddings of rice and figs.

I have already mentioned the agricultural emphasis in the county's public-house names, but country matters of an earthy flavour are also hinted at in The Maidenhead which occurs more than once, coyly restyled Maiden's Head these days; and at Whitwell, lying, as it were, in the lap of Hertfordshire, one of those once-popular cautionary verses, using the names of local pubs to warn children against the evils inside, contained the unwitting *double-entendre*:

> The Maiden's Head has often led
> Young people in to sin.

King's Walden and St Paul's Walden are tiny villages which have both made their contributions to English history, despite being perhaps the first truly rural parishes we have so far reached in the county – a view which is borne out by the number of ghost stories told there.

Lieutenant-Colonel John Hale was a member of that Hale

family which followed the King as lords of the manor of King's Walden and remained there until the early years of this century. Many of their memorials can be seen in the church. The Colonel raised a regiment of Hertfordshire men, mainly from this district, to fight against the French with General Wolfe, and 'Hale's Dragoons' later became the 17th Lancers, who took part in the famous charge of the Light Brigade.

St Paul's Walden was once known as Abbot's Walden (like the Langleys, one village was owned by the King and the other by the Abbot of St Albans). Here in 1900, at St Paul's Walden Bury, between the village and Whitwell, was born a daughter of the Earl and Countess of Strathmore. She was Lady Elizabeth Bowes-Lyon, who married the Duke of York and became Queen of England when he was crowned George VI, and survived him to become Queen Elizabeth, the much-loved Queen Mother.

Preston, a peaceful and attractive village, was owned by the Knights Templars, whose preceptory, Temple Dinsley, eventually passed to the Sadleir family and then to one Benedict Ithell, who built a new mansion on the site. This in turn was enlarged and modernized by Lutyens and became a college. Another building in the village which disguises a historic site is Castle Farm. An earlier building here was called Hunsdon House, and the Foster brothers who lived there gave shelter to a Protestant preacher who delivered his sermons to congregations gathered at midnight in the secrecy of nearby Wain Wood. No one could have been surprised by the preacher's arrest and imprisonment, but who would have guessed that he would be the author of one of the great works in English literature? His name was John Bunyan.

Later, Hunsdon House was bought by Captain Robert Hinde of the Light Dragoons, who embattled it and called it Preston Castle, from where he enlisted troops of children and farmworkers to march to Hitchin, accompanied by drums and trumpets, in some extravagant military ritual which got him known as the General, though his official rank remained more modest. It is sometimes said that Laurence Sterne based his character Uncle Toby, in *Tristram Shandy*, on Captain Hinde, for Uncle Toby studies the art of war on his bowling green, aided and abetted by the faithful Corporal Trim.

Lilley and Great Offley lie close together on the road between Luton and Hitchin, in attractive farming country where splendid views across Bedfordshire can be seen; one of them being from Telegraph Hill, so called because a signalling station was maintained there during the Napoleonic War.

Lilley was the home of an eccentric named Johann Kellerman, who has been called "the last of the alchemists", but he was no ancient, bent and bearded fellow. Sir Richard Phillips, the nineteenth-century journalist, visited this man who was reputed to have discovered the Philosopher's Stone, and found a six-foot fellow of athletic build, with black and rolling eyes, who protected his property with barricades and man-traps.

Offley is held to be the burial place of Offa, Saxon King of Mercia and founder of St Albans Abbey, but we are hardly likely to be convinced of that by the inscription on two fourteenth-century tiles in the church, declaring, with unfathomable logic, that they were found in 1777, "which proves that King Offa was buried here".

I feel less inclined to argue with the weightier evidence that Sir Thomas and Lady Salusbury were buried here. Their monument by Nollekens overwhelms the chancel, built by Sir Thomas in the eighteenth century, and the real treasure of this village church is the more modest font, which some medieval craftsman carved with beautiful tracery. Hester Lynch Salusbury, who – as we have noted – married into the Thrale family and became Dr Johnson's friend, was the niece of Sir Thomas, and she later recalled Offley as "the place I earliest attached my silly heart to".

The scattered hamlets in this parish and its vicinity, with typical Hertfordshire names like Tea Green and Wandon End, are so close to the eastward crawl of Luton that they cannot long survive as rural hamlets. Within a stone's throw of Luton Airport, their solitude is already shattered by the roar of jet aircraft, and the signs of their ruin have already been posted. But there are some attractive spots here yet, with tiny hamlets scattered about the slightly larger villages with their little greens and churches, the Ends justifying the Greens, as it were.

Beyond the Icknield Way the villages which concern us in this chapter are Hexton and Pirton, forming a crab-like claw with a peninsular bit of Bedfordshire in its grip. I have already mentioned the prehistoric earthwork near Hexton called Ravensburgh Castle, and further evidence of the ancient influences at work in this village is provided by Francis Taverner, a lord of the manor whose relations are commemorated in the church, which has the unusual dedication to St Faith.

Here, as in other places, Hock-tide festivities took place, Taverner tells us, to celebrate the end of Danish occupation, and lasted until the reign of Elizabeth I. Men and women went to the top of Wayting Hill on Hock Monday (second after Easter) and the women pulled down a pole of ash which had been erected for the purpose there, and strove to get it to the bottom of the hill, while the men had to try to keep it at the top. A lusty battle thus ensued, during which the men were apt to let go suddenly so that the women all fell over. But the gradient of the hill was on the women's side, and having successfully brought the pole down they took it to the town hall, where all ate and drank together, and money was collected for the repair of the church and bells. This device of superimposing a Christian motive on a pagan ceremony is one with which the British people have hoodwinked the Church for centuries. Then in the afternoon more riotous sport took place, when the women,

> if they toke any of the weaker men prisoners they would use them unhapilye inoughe. I think these nicer tymes of ours would not only despise these sports, but also account them ymodest if not prophane. But those playne and well meaning people did solace themselves in this manner, and that without offence or scandall.

There are some fine old houses in and around Pirton, among which High Down, south of the village, was the home of the influential Docwra family, one of whom established a penny post in London. A headless cavalier, killed here by Cromwell's soldiers, is said to ride from High Down to Hitchin Priory once a year, on the night of 15 June. I have never seen him; nor have I observed the glint of the gold supposed to be at the bottom of Pirton Pond, but this is not the only legend of buried treasure at Pirton, so perhaps there is something in it.

The moated Pirton Grange, north-west of the village, is tucked tightly into the corner of Hertfordshire. The home of the Hanscombs, one of the family's eighteenth-century members, James, attached to his account book an almanac which contains the advice for October: "The garments you last month hung on your backs in jest, now button them in good earnest." Well, it is October as I write these lines, and I feel disposed to button up in good earnest before returning south to face the far more chilling prospect of the Great North Road.

VI

THE WAY OF ALL FLESH

THE A1 thunders into the county just south of the point where the A6 joins it near Ridge. Surging forward with a snakelike thrust, it becomes a motorway, A1(M), after a few miles, weaving its way between the New Towns of Hatfield, Welwyn Garden City, Stevenage and Letchworth, and leaving Hertfordshire beyond the village of Radwell on its long journey north to Edinburgh.

This is the much-changed Great North Road, once romantic, then notorious, now monstrous. In the days of the stage-coach it featured in the novels of Dickens and Jane Austen; it was the happy hunting ground of Dick Turpin; it was belaboured by Defoe for its impassable state. A typical incident was the theft of the mail for Hatfield, Welwyn, Stevenage and Baldock in March 1810. Robbers forced off the lock whilst the horses were being changed at Barnet. The milestones along the route, set up in Defoe's time, were among the first in Britain since those of the Roman occupation. Since the advent of the internal combustion engine, the road has made an appearance in the novels of J. B. Priestley and Dorothy L. Sayers, and been branded as "the bloodiest country lane in Europe" for the number of accidents caused by its hazardous bends. But it was the premier highway of Britain, and when roads were classified in the 1920s, all the others had this - the A1 - as their standard and bearing.

Now, diverted, widened, rebuilt, modernized, the A1(M) is not recognizable as the former Great North Road, which went through Potters Bar, Old Hatfield and Baldock. In fact, the Hertfordshire stretch of the road consists almost entirely of bypasses, built to miss first Barnet, then Hatfield, then Welwyn, then Stevenage and finally Baldock. It carries a colossal amount of traffic, some of it heavy, most of it fast, and all of it noisy, into and out of London at all times of the day and night, the north-bound vehicles roaring out from Mill Hill and Edgware to blaze a fiery trail through the centre of Hertfordshire.

Formerly the road entered the county near Borehamwood and left it again momentarily to cross the Middlesex tongue in which lay Potters Bar, but the burnt offering of Barnet at the high altar of London expansion meant that Hertfordshire lost about two and a half miles of the A1 as well – a very satisfactory bargain!

South and North Mymms are first to suffer the London exodus on this route. The southern village is strictly spelt Mimms, as both were once, and though it is small, its parish used to include all Potters Bar and much surrounding countryside. South Mimms came to Hertfordshire with Potters Bar in 1965, its ancient church of St Giles being one of the county's more interesting acquisitions in the deal.

North Mymms contains, on one side of the A1, North Mymms Park, and on the other, Brookmans Park, the latter having given its name to a sizeable residential estate, to the north-east of which is the BBC's extensive wireless transmitting station. North Mymms House stands in the former park, probably on the site of the medieval village which has disappeared. Possibly Sir Ralph Coningsby, who built the E-shaped mansion of red brick in 1599, moved the populace and demolished the village in order to acquire a desirable estate. We do not really know. At any rate, the house eventually passed to the Duke of Leeds, and subsequently became well known for its paintings by Bellini, Breughel and Reynolds, among others, and for its rose gardens by William Robinson.

Brookmans was built by Baron Somers of Evesham, William III's wise Lord Chancellor, to whom Swift, then in the service of Sir William Temple at the Surrey 'Moor Park', inscribed the dedication of his *Tale of a Tub*, saying: "Your lordship's name on the front in capital letters will at any time get off one edition." Lord Somers died here in 1716, and his marble monument is in the parish church of St Mary, which stands in the grounds of North Mymms Park. A later owner of Brookmans, in order to extend the park, demolished a house called Gobions, which had once been the property of Sir Thomas More. It is sometimes said that he wrote *Utopia* there, but there is no firm evidence for that. The house was soon followed into oblivion by its upstart neighbour, for in 1891 Brookmans was burnt to the ground.

Potters Bar is the first stop in the so-called Green Belt on the line from King's Cross, so it is a commuter centre, swept along by the irresistible tide of city gents coming ashore from their daily plunge into the deep waters of central London. The 'Bar' comes from the fact that the village once had a turnpike gate on the Great North Road. The rapid growth in its size and population with the coming of the railway in the nineteenth century made it deserving of a church of its own, and buried in the churchyard are thirty-five men who formed the crews of two Zeppelin airships which were shot down nearby during the First World War.

Northaw, a pleasant little village standing above the northern reaches of Enfield Chase, has a curious legend about a hermit named Sigar who lived there in the twelfth century. It seems he walked the twelve miles to St Albans Abbey every night to join Matins at three o'clock in the morning, and spent his days in prayer and meditation. But he was regularly disturbed by the singing of nightingales, so he prayed that they should be removed, and when his prayers were answered, a hermit at Markyate sought his aid in banishing the birds from that village, too. No doubt some local ornithologist could give us evidence that the divine ban on nightingales in the area has not lasted.

We come to Hatfield next, and overriding all other considerations in this town and its surroundings is the greatest stately home in Hertfordshire and, indeed, one of the greatest in England, standing on high ground overlooking the old town and directly opposite the railway station (no unworldly country estate, this). The magnificent red-brick Jacobean mansion of Hatfield House was built early in the seventeenth century by Robert Cecil, the first Earl of Salisbury, and Chief Minister of State under Queen Elizabeth and James I. But in order to have a proper understanding of this great house and its great family, we must go back a little further in time, for the original house here was called Hatfield Palace, and it was completed in 1497 for the Bishop of Ely on land which had been owned by his predecessors since the eleventh century, and had earned the village the name Bishop's Hatfield. Before long, however, Henry VIII took it over and deposited his children there – Elizabeth, Mary and Edward. Elizabeth was in residence – reading under an oak tree in the park – when she was proclaimed Queen after the deaths of her half-brother Edward VI and her sister Mary Tudor. She called upon William Cecil to be her chief minister, and held her first council in the Hall of Hatfield Palace, leaving it soon after to return only rarely.

Sir William Cecil, later Lord Burghley, was one of the most dedicated servants of the state England has ever had. A lawyer and classical scholar, he belonged to a Protestant family which had its home at Stamford in Lincolnshire, and which had been loyal to the Crown since the advent of the Tudor dynasty after the Battle of Bosworth. William Cecil served Queen Elizabeth as her adviser, chief minister and Lord Treasurer for forty years, until the day of his death, by which time he had established his family name as one of the foremost in England.

Burleigh had built a large house in a park called Theobalds, near Cheshunt and forming part of Enfield Chase, and there he lived with his family, and there he died. His son Robert succeeded him as the Queen's first minister, and after Elizabeth's death, served James I. In 1607, James offered Robert Cecil the Royal Palace of Hatfield and other extensive properties in exchange for Theobalds, which he coveted as a hunting lodge. How could Cecil refuse his master without risking the loss of his position and the royal favour? He agreed, and James made him Earl of Salisbury into the bargain. Robert immediately set about building a new mansion, the Hatfield House we see today, using materials from the greater part of the old Palace which he demolished, leaving only its

Great Hall intact. The house cost £40,000 and was completed in 1612, but by that time Robert Cecil was dead.

The house inherited by his descendants was built to the E-plan design of Robert Lyminge, and is a most impressive place, as full of treasures in its architecture and decoration as in its content and history (as well as trivia like Queen Elizabeth's silk stockings). One has only to enter the Marble Hall, with its sumptuous woodcarving, minstrels' gallery, Flemish tapestries, and portraits of Elizabeth and Mary Queen of Scots, to feel that one has stepped into an age that was at once more elegant, more intellectual and more stylish than the one left outside on the former Great North Road.

Yet Robert Cecil, though an able politician, was not the equal of his father Lord Burghley, and he made enemies. Hunchbacked and sickly, he was the target for libellous jibes and his building the object of criticism by the local populace, who claimed that he had illegally enclosed part of Hatfield woods. Later in the century, a local bigwig, Sir Francis Boteler, exercised his right of passage through what he claimed was an ancient public right of way, by riding his horse up the north steps, through Hatfield House and out the other side.

By that time, there was a marked strain of eccentricity running through the Cecils themselves. When Samuel Pepys visited Hatfield he was much more impressed by the size of the earl's gooseberries than by "my simple Lord Salisbury", and the Cecils from the second to the sixth earls were an undistinguished lot, presiding over a steady decline in the family's fortune and importance. The sixth Earl fancied himself as a stage-coach driver, and actually undertook the job occasionally, thus earning the unwonted immortality of a line – like Styles at Moor Park – in Pope's satires.

With the seventh Earl, things began to look up, and as Lord David Cecil has made clear, this was due at least as much to the countess as to the Earl himself. James Cecil married Lady Emily Mary Hill, a beautiful and flamboyant woman who soon made herself the most famous society hostess in the land and injected a fresh dose of eccentricity into the family blood. Her portrait by Sir Joshua Reynolds is one of the finest in the house. In 1789 George III made the seventh Earl Marquess of Salisbury for his loyalty to the Crown, the excessive degree of which is well illustrated by the Duchess of Devonshire's observation that, when the King was rightly supposed by the court and the whole nation to be out of his mind, "Lord Salisbury says the King has as much sence as he has." But the title, the domination of Hatfield by the Marchioness, and the Cecils' position as leaders of the Tory aristocracy, set the family fortunes on the road to recovery, notwithstanding the notoriety of the Marchioness in her later years.

After her husband's death, she became widely known as "Dowager Sal" or "Old Sarum". Her beauty long gone, her face was described by Creevey as "the most cracked, or rather furrowed piece of mosaic you have ever saw", but well into her eighties, she attended balls, played cards late into the night, incurred huge gambling debts, and even hunted, strapped to her horse and told when to jump by her groom who rode beside her. Never sharing the deep religious convictions of the family she had married into, she held concerts at Hatfield on Sunday evenings which proved more powerful attractions than the services in the parish church, not only to the parishioners invited, but to the rector himself. Once, arriving at church to find it full, one of her daughters asked her where they should go, to which the old lady promptly replied: "Home again, to be sure." Finally, she accidentally set fire to her bedroom and died as spectacularly as she had lived, in the blaze which consumed the whole west wing of the house. Among the newspaper reporters who witnessed the scene was Charles Dickens.

With due respect to the Dowager Marchioness's son, the second Marquess, who rebuilt the west wing, redesigned parts of the gardens, and welcomed the railway, it is her grandson Robert, the third Marquess, who must claim our special attention, for he was the first great man to bear the name of Cecil since the days of Lord Burghley and his son. Robert Cecil, third Marquess of Salisbury, Knight of the Garter,

Fellow of All Souls', Chancellor of the University of Oxford, leader of the Conservative Party, and three times Prime Minister of England during the period of its greatest prestige and power, was born at Hatfield House in 1830, and was, I think, the greatest man ever born on Hertfordshire soil. His character has been so well described by Lord David Cecil, and his political career so fully analysed by his biographers, that there is no need to expand on them at any length here. But a man who could be admired as much by a twentieth-century atheist as by Queen Victoria, must have possessed a remarkable variety of qualities which I must try to summarize.

For my own part, one of the keys to his appeal is his remark to his daughter-in-law who was upset by the failure of a good cause she had supported. "Surely this failure matters very much," she said. "My dear," Lord Salisbury replied, "nothing matters *very* much." What a superbly cosmic view of the insignificance of man, in one whose profession compelled him to pretend that the fate of the world hinged on the shape of a conference table. A born sceptic, he distrusted experts, was deeply suspicious of democracy, and kept clear of humanity in the mass, though he and the Marchioness dutifully entertained at Hatfield guests as diverse as the Shah of Persia and Lewis Carroll. (As well as being a statesman, Lord Salisbury was something of a scientist, and if the reader hears a sizzle whilst scanning this sentence, it is only because the naked wires, by means of which His Lordship has installed electric light in Hatfield House, have suddenly burst into flames on the ceiling. Lord Salisbury, interrupted in conversation, nonchalantly throws up a cushion to extinguish the fire, and carries on talking . . .)

A statue of the third Marquess now stands, or rather sits, at the gates of Hatfield House, facing the railway station and looking, it has often been whimsically suggested, as if he were waiting for a train. Inside the house, however, if there is one picture more arresting than the Reynolds portrait of his grandmother, it is George Richmond's portrait of the Marquess in the robes of the Chancellor of Oxford, in middle age, looking for all the world, with his black beard and penetrating eyes, like Dostoevsky. And in fact while Dostoevsky was losing money at the roulette tables of Wiesbaden, Lord Salisbury, the Prime Minister of England, was refused admission to the Casino at Monte Carlo because he looked like a tramp – he was always careless of his clothes and appearance.

Clearly these were not the characteristics which made him appeal to Queen Victoria. His oratorical power and his efficiency in office were equally attractive, and his policy was always "to abstain from a meddling diplomacy, to uphold England's honour steadily and fearlessly, and always to be prone rather to let action go along with words than to let it lag behind them". His success in these aims led the Queen to offer him a dukedom, but he refused it, and died at Hatfield House seventy-three years after his birth there, having begotten five sons who were well able to uphold the proud name of Cecil; the eldest becoming fourth Marquess, another becoming Bishop of Exeter and another winning the Nobel Peace Prize.

The large thirteenth-century parish church of St Etheldreda, Hatfield, contains the Salisbury Chapel (built 1618) in which is the tomb of Robert Cecil, the first Earl, whose effigy is supported by the figures of women representing Faith, Justice, Fortitude and Prudence, the four cardinal virtues, "in virgin habits", as the old writers were apt to put it, "and with their proper attributes". (Arthur Mee referred to them curiously as "white women", as if he was surprised they are not negresses!) The attributes of one of them (not Prudence, surely) include bare breasts which are, as Pevsner says, "a reminder of the distance which European civilization had travelled between the time when the church and when the chapel was built". The monument was ordered from Simon Basyll, Surveyor of the King's Works, who submitted an estimate to the second Earl of £460, including carving the figures which "if they be done according to art and true proportion, are worth £60 a piece". The figures were made by Maximilian Colt. There are also monuments to the third Marquess and to Lord Melbourne – three prime ministers in one former village church.

Hatfield is now one of Hertfordshire's thriving New Towns, and as all these, apart from Hemel Hempstead, are spread along the course of the A1, it will be convenient to bring them together here. They are Letchworth, Stevenage, Hatfield and Welwyn Garden City.

Town planning has occupied the thinking of men as great and as far back in time as Aristotle and Leonardo da Vinci, but the original prophet of the English New Towns, who took the brave step of putting his ideas into practice, was Sir Ebenezer Howard, and no one has had a greater effect than he upon the appearance of modern Hertfordshire. Born in London, he emigrated to the United States when he was twenty, but returned four years later and worked as a newspaper reporter. Shocked by the overcrowding and slums in London, he wrote a book called *Tomorrow: a Peaceful Path to Real Reform*, in which he envisaged towns set among trees and lawns and surrounded by agricultural belts - pleasant to live in, convenient to work in, and to a large extent self-sufficient.

In 1903 Howard and his associates set up a limited company called First Garden City Ltd and began to build a town on this model on a site acquired at Letchworth. At first, its growth was very slow. Capital was short, industry was unenthusiastic about moving thirty-five miles from London and the whole scheme was ridiculed as fantastic and eccentric. But it did grow, and much of Howard's plan was achieved, Letchworth now being a major industrial town in which the factories do not impose themselves depressingly on the well-designed residential areas. The growth of industry was carefully controlled so that a balanced need for male and female workers, and skilled and unskilled labour, was created, and the huge variety of work there includes engineering and food production, printing and furniture manufacture. Letchworth was also built as a 'dry' town, and it remained so despite occasional referendums - its lack of public houses making it in yet another sense a curiously uncharacteristic bit of Hertfordshire.

Letchworth soon lost its suffix 'Garden City', but Welwyn Garden City, Howard's second venture, has retained it to distinguish the town from old Welwyn, which remains a separate village, to the eternal confusion of telephone operators everywhere. The name was controversial even in the early stages, but a plebiscite held in 1924 showed a majority in favour of retaining it, and as the alternatives on offer included such brilliant ideas as Handside and Welwyn South, I am not surprised!

Welwyn Garden City was begun after the First World War, and was carefully planned to avoid such mistakes as experience had showed up at Letchworth. Ebenezer Howard was knighted in 1927, and he died at Welwyn Garden City in the following year, but with the satisfaction of having turned a dream of Utopia into a sort of practical reality, for which the world was in his debt. Town planning experts came from Russia and America to see his achievements, which set a pattern for all the New Towns built since.

In 1948, Welwyn Garden City was taken over by a government development corporation under the New Towns Act, and the town is now being administered in conjunction with neighbouring Hatfield, which had begun to expand more spontaneously with the coming of the De Havilland Aircraft Company in 1930 - an event that led to the building, three years later, of the Comet, which Pevsner says is "one of the earliest inns in England built in the style of the C20, without borrowings from the past".

De Havilland's aircraft built at Hatfield included the fast and versatile wooden Mosquito, designed at Salisbury Hall, and the later Comet civil airliner. This was the world's first pure-jet airliner, and it made its maiden flight from Hatfield in 1949, piloted by the company's chief test pilot, Group Captain John Cunningham, who had in the previous year established a new altitude record over Hertfordshire in the firm's Vampire aircraft. In 1960, the De Havilland company was absorbed into the mammoth Hawker Siddeley group, and two years later the first Trident aircraft took off from Hatfield on its maiden flight. This famous airliner was the first to introduce automatic landing in regular service, with British European Airways, who showed that it could operate when other aircraft were grounded by bad visibility. Tridents have since been built in vast numbers at Hatfield for airlines throughout the world.

Stevenage had the doubtful honour of being the first town developed entirely under the New Towns Act, and it was the scene of a bitterly fought action, which reached the House of Lords, to prevent it from happening at all, for Stevenage was a busy little town of character with an ancient history, its name coming from the burial mounds known as the Six Hills – the Saxon *stigenhaght.* Old Stevenage did not have an altogether happy reputation in some quarters in the eighteenth century, however. As one local poet put it:

> Long noted Stevenage, where the Mothers bawl
> And to the Scorpion brood, poor things, they call;
> Turnips and Gate posts they are taught to steal,
> Soon as the Pap within their mouths they feel . . .

There was an "Association of the Gentlemen, Farmers and other inhabitants of the parish and neighbourhood of Stevenage in the County of Hertford for apprehending and prosecuting Felons and Thieves of all denominations" – including, presumably, marauding gangs of swaddled infants who stole out at dead of night and tore up gateposts!

The growth of Stevenage in the late 'fifties was very much in step with the age. Instead of the old-world look of Letchworth and the neo-Georgian style of Welwyn Garden City, concrete is much in evidence here, and a Henry Moore sculpture 'The Family' stands at the entrance of the large Barclay School, while the new parish church has a bell-tower which looks like a rocket. The day the vicar announces hymn number two, one, zero, we shall have lift-off for heaven, I suspect. This is not entirely inappropriate, for Stevenage has been nicknamed Space City since the British Aircraft Corporation built the Blue Streak rockets here that provided the thrust for Britain's original space programme. The Blue Streak had originally been designed at Hatfield by De Havillands as a military weapon to carry a thermo-nuclear warhead.

The aircraft and aero-dynamics industries at Hatfield and

Stevenage have accounted for a considerable share of the population growth in these post-war New Towns, which might suggest that they are more of the twentieth century in outlook than Letchworth and Welwyn Garden City. But their advantages and their drawbacks are perhaps identical in this sense: that they (as well as Hemel Hempstead) have not existed in their new form long enough to have developed any real community identity. Instant Utopias are not possible now - probably never were possible, human nature being what it is - and what have been well called 'New Town Blues' have afflicted all of them to some degree.

This is not the fault of the planners. It is one of the growing pains of a new town peopled with uneasy strangers torn from their familiar surroundings and deprived of the comfortable feeling of belonging. It will disappear when the towns are old enough to have borne two or three generations of natives, and old men who have lived here all their lives can sit on the park benches discussing how it all started, or recalling the coolest winter on record, or the drought of '76. Too many young mothers occupy the park benches at present.

In the meantime, the strange kind of void in which the new communities exist has been blamed for, among other things, an alarming degree of drug-taking among young people in Welwyn Garden City. But signs of approaching normality are already there. In *The Lore and Language of Schoolchildren*, Iona and Peter Opie cited Welwyn Garden City as one of the places where children practise a ritual called "breaking the cross", in which a child will uphold his code of honour by crossing his fingers and saying: "Break my cross if I tell a lie." Thus the growth of a local tradition takes place in a town only half a century old, and the offspring of that generation will take Stevenage, Letchworth, Welwyn Garden City and Hatfield, no longer called New Towns by that time, very much for granted.

Essendon, set in attractive country to the east of Hatfield, is notable for the benefits bestowed upon it by those two formidable industrialists Josiah Wedgwood and Samuel Whitbread. The classically designed font in the church is of

Wedgwood black basalt ware, and Whitbread, who owned Bedwell Park south of the village, rebuilt many of the old houses in Essendon. Camfield Place, nearby, offers a startling contrast to this impression of industrial patriarchy of a rural community. It was built by Edmund Potter, whose grand-daughter Beatrix wrote her first rabbit story there, within sight of Warren Wood. Now, Camfield Place is the home of another story-teller, the honey-and-vitamin pundit Barbara Cartland.

Lemsford, lying perilously close to the A1(M), has the surprising distinction of having been called by Queen Elizabeth (the first, not the second) "the prettiest village in England". Another surprise here is the nineteenth-century village church, unusual in Hertfordshire in being built of stone instead of flint. And hardly less surprising is the variety of explanations offered for the name of the inn, Long Arm and Short Arm. One says it means the 'arms' put out to indicate to travellers deep or shallow water in the ford they had to cross; another that it was due to the two approach roads to the realigned Great North Road which, before 1833, ran through the village centre; and, most improbably, that the horse painter and former coachman G. F. Herring painted the original sign for it showing a customer stretching out his arm for a tankard of ale held close by the publican.

Nor have we finished with Lemsford's surprises yet. If all the foregoing seems a bit unlikely in the shadow of a motorway and on the threshold of a new garden city, what of Lemsford Mill, which is said to have inspired J. P. Skelly to write that justly popular and long-lasting old romantic song:

> There's an old mill by the stream,
> Nelly Dean,
> Where we used to sit and dream,
> Nelly Dean,
> And the waters as they flow
> Seem to murmur soft and low,
> You're my heart's desire, I love you,
> Nelly Dean.

The mill is still there, but if you can hear the water above the roar of traffic, it seems to be choking for breath rather than murmuring soft and low, and it is a little easier to believe the more intellectual love affair recalled by the large estate across the river, for Brocket Hall was the home of that extraordinary woman, Lady Caroline Lamb. Brocket Park had been owned by the Lamb family since about 1746, and Sir Matthew Lamb began work on building a new mansion and landscaping the grounds in 1775. His son Sir Peniston became the first Viscount Melbourne, who sat in Parliament for forty years without embarking on his maiden speech. Peniston's son William was not so slow. In 1806 he married Caroline Ponsonby, the daughter of the Earl and Countess of Bessborough, and became Whig M.P. for Leominster. But he had to contend with the sensational behaviour of his neurotic wife and suffer her death before he could achieve his own fame as Queen Victoria's first Prime Minister.

Caroline Lamb, thin, lisping and tomboyish with her unfashionable short haircut, was clever, provocative and exotic, hated by her own sex but pursued by many men, among whom was the ridiculous Prince of Wales, who tearfully implored her to become his mistress three years after her marriage. But she was hopelessly infatuated with Lord Byron, whom she drove almost to distraction with her unwonted attentions. Once when he had repulsed her, Caroline's hysterical exhibitionism led her to have a huge fire lit in the grounds of Brocket Hall for a sort of pagan ritual in which she dressed village girls in white to dance round the flames while she recited an elegy of her own composition and burned Byron's portrait. There was worse to come. She turned up at a society function at which Byron was present, and gashed her arms with a broken glass and a pair of scissors. And although afterwards she sent him a 'sensible' letter and some Hertfordshire gooseberries, she may well have been responsible for the rumours of incest that ruined Byron's reputation and sent him abroad for the rest of his life.

Meanwhile, her long-suffering and over-tolerant husband had agreed to a separation, but when solicitors arrived with the necessary papers they found the couple, to say the least, reconciled – Caroline sitting on William's knee and feeding him with bread and butter. Then, some years later, she was driving out of Brocket Park when a funeral cortège passed the gates. Enquiring who the dead person was, Lady Caroline was told that it was Lord Byron, and she fainted, her mind becoming permanently unhinged until her death not long afterwards.

William Lamb, freed from this outrageous liability, now began his rise to power, becoming second Viscount Melbourne when his father died, then Home Secretary and in 1834, Prime Minister. Queen Victoria became emotionally attached to this man whom she regarded as "truly honest, straightforward and noble-minded". He did not appear so to others, for he was the villain of the piece in the affair of the Tolpuddle Martyrs, and he had financial interests in coal mines in which children worked a fourteen-hour day. But fortunately for himself, perhaps, he had a nice sense of humour, and once said: "Things have come to a pretty pass when religion is allowed to invade the sphere of private life".

When Lord Melbourne died in 1848, his only child, Lady Caroline's epileptic son, was already long dead, so the Brocket estate passed to his sister Emily, who had married Earl Cowper of Panshanger, but had children by Lord Palmerston while her husband was alive, and married their father when her husband was dead. Lord Palmerston himself became Prime Minister twice, lived at Brocket Hall, and died there whilst in office, by which time – so far from being the noted seducer of the ladies-in-waiting at Windsor, for which he had been nicknamed Cupid – Disraeli had uncharitably described him as "an old pantaloon, very deaf, very blind and with false teeth, which would fall out of his mouth when speaking if he did not hesitate and halt so much in his talk".

The best view of Brocket Hall is obtained from the fine wrought-iron gates near the Crooked Chimney public house on the old Great North Road (now A6129) just beyond Lemsford, and at the next right turn, the old Roman road takes you, via a ford, to the delightfully open and unspoiled Ayot Green.

Another large house in the area is Lockleys at Welwyn, built in 1717, which became the home of the eccentric scientist George Dering, who was responsible for supplying the first gas to the surrounding villages in 1860. Dering entertained at Lockleys a friend of his named Jean-François Gravelet, who used the Mimram valley nearby to practise a stunt he was planning to undertake in America. The 35-year-old Frenchman won world fame when he carried out his plan successfully, walking a tightrope across Niagara Falls blindfold, pushing a wheelbarrow, and carrying a man on his back, under the stage name Charles Blondin.

The little River Mimram is only a trickling stream, but a few years before Blondin's feat, the engineers of the Great Northern Railway had already found it necessary to build a viaduct to take the line across the "impassable barrier" of the river's valley of soft clay. The forty brick arches are 100 feet high and carry the railway a distance of about 1,500 feet, and writers on Hertfordshire generally open the filing cabinets of their vocabularies and pull out all the superlatives when mentioning the Digswell Viaduct, describing it as "mighty", "gigantic" and "a wonder". But that is only because your typical Hertfordshire man is London-orientated, and has never been just up the road to Northamptonshire to see the Welland Viaduct, which has twice the Digswell's number of arches and more than double its length. Cussans wrote: "To say that Digswell is the prettiest place in Hertfordshire may be considered as a bold assertion." It may indeed! The railway and the viaduct were already there when he wrote, so we cannot find excuses for his perverse judgement. Perhaps he saw it on a sunny afternoon after a particularly hearty lunch.

Bramfield might be considered a prettier place today, especially when one sees the village post office – a delightful thatched cottage with tall chimneys and latticed windows set in a garden of roses with a background of trees. More interesting than the old legend that Bramfield was Thomas à Becket's first parish is the fact that here at Bacon's Farm lived

John Carrington, little known outside the county, whose diary, in breathless unpunctuated prose, is a mine of information about local people, events and customs.

In 1801 he conducted the first local census, and found in Bramfield that there were 91 males and 101 "fea males" living in 28 houses. In 1805, he reported to his diary that: "Monday 20th about 2 Clock in afternoon one of Esqr Searanks Great Casks at Hatfield Brewer Busted of 535 Barrels in the stoor House 3 of the Bottom hoops flew and the Beer Run Down the water Corse to the River from Hatfield being quite full of the Best Beer 535 Barrls the Loss supposed to be £1000".

1809 was occasion for Bramfield to celebrate:

> To Bramfield to the Jubilee Given by the Parish to the Poor of the Parish, and to all the Farmers Servants Do. and other Poor that Work in the Parish, on Account of George the third King Entring the 50th year of his Reign on the 25th of this Month. Given 3 Rounds, one Aich Bone, 2 Mouse Buttoks of Beef, 2 Shoulders, one Legg, 2 Necks of Mutton, 4 Sewitt pudings and Plumb Dumplings, 20 quartan Loves, 1 Bush of Carrotts, 1 Bush of Turnops, 1 Bush of puttatoes, + plenty of Table Beer with their Dinner, and after Dinner Each man and woman 1 quart of Strong Beer Each and the Children, 1 pint each.

A man and a woman who died within a few years of each other at Tewin were commemorated in the one case by a tablet in the church and in the other by a wooden post at the side of the road, the latter being symbolic of the stake which was driven through the body of the notorious footpad Walter Clibborn, who was shot dead just after Christmas in 1782. The Chief Constable of the Liberty of St Albans recorded the death "about 30 pole from Okenvaley Bottom towards Bull Green". The stake was driven through the corpse to keep him down, and it is a wonder they did not do the same with the woman who died there seven years later.

Elizabeth Malyn, the daughter of a brewer, married the local lord of the manor, but he died within a few years, and she then married Colonel Sabine of Queen Hoo Hall, who died even more speedily, to be followed into his widow's bed by Lord Cathcart, who did not survive two years. Lady

Cathcart then married an unscrupulous Irishman named Macguire, who had every intention of surviving her and getting her fortune, and to this end imprisoned her in his Irish castle for twenty years. Her enforced patience was rewarded, however, for Macguire was killed in a duel and his widow came back to Tewin. She said of her marriages that "the first was to please my parents, the second for money, the third for a title and the fourth because the Devil owed me a grudge". She wore a ring which she had inscribed "If I survive I'll make it five", but she wanted to enjoy herself a bit after her long ordeal in Ireland, and she danced the years away and then died before she had fixed on a fifth husband. She was ninety-seven.

"Procrastination is the thief of time," as Rev. Edward Young, the rector of Welwyn, had written for our eternal quotation whilst Lady Cathcart was briefly wed to His Lordship. Young, the author of *Night Thoughts*, who attempted to turn Welwyn into a spa, is commemorated by a monument in Welwyn's church of St Mary, beneath a much rebuilt tower. The original tower had collapsed in a severe storm in the seventeenth century, and the subsequent one, built of brick in 1834 to replace a bell turret, was called "hideous" by Cussans, and was evidently thought so by others:

> Oh, the foolish Welwyn people,
> Sold their bells to buy a steeple.

This notorious brick-built tower was seen by Vincent Van Gogh, who spent some time in England in his early years (with his faculties and ears intact). He visited his sister at Welwyn, where she taught at a school near the church, since converted into a cottage. Early in this century, the tower was again rebuilt, and is now solid and ordinary.

Old Welwyn, as it is popularly called (especially by telephonists!), has a dearth of helpful road signs, but if you can find your way out of it to the west, you come to the villages of Ayot St Peter and Ayot St Lawrence, the latter having once been known as Great Ayot, though smaller than Ayot St Peter. Perhaps they anticipated the arrival of the man who was to make Ayot St Lawrence famous throughout the civilized world.

I am anticipating him myself, to be sure, for we must first consider other aspects of these villages, which are set amid abundant cornfields and narrow lanes in a very appealing part of the county, although—according to Nathaniel Salmon—the name Ayot comes from "Ayest, a Desert, or wild uncultivated Place". Modern scholars take a different guess, dreaming up another of those all-purpose Saxons for us to believe in if we choose.

When Salmon wrote his history, there was nothing for him to remark about the church of Ayot St Lawrence except its antiquities and its incumbent, Rev. Samuel Hassel. Less than 150 years later, however, it was in ruins, and Cussans had much to say about it. The story goes that the owner of the newly built Ayot House, on the north side of the village, found the church obstructing his hilltop view, and as it was (so he alleged) in a ruinous state, he decided to demolish it and build a new one. He was the lord of the manor, Sir Lionel Lyde, and he did not wait for ecclesiastical approval of his plan, but the Bishop intervened when demolition was already under way, and although the pulling down of the church proceeded no further, it was never rebuilt, and it is now a picturesque ruin.

Meanwhile, Sir Lionel had engaged Nicholas Revett to design a church to be built in his own grounds, half a mile away, in the Greek style, and it was this "heathen temple" that Cussans found so offensive, taking Lyde to task for making a "public exhibition of his wealth and his folly" by erecting what Cussans saw as "simply a disgrace to the disgraceful period of British ecclesiastical taste in which it was built". Perhaps he was right, but I have to confess a sneaking admiration for this little classical building which you approach across a field from the village centre.

In 1948, a pair of new wrought-iron gates was placed at the entrance to the old churchyard from the village street, and the man who was invited to unveil them told the villagers: "This is His house, this is His gate, and this is His way". Nothing very unusual about that, we may think, particularly when the speaker was the occupant of the New Rectory. But in fact the speaker was Ayot St Lawrence's most famous resident, the 92-year-old sage George Bernard Shaw, who was dead within two years, leaving in his will a more characteristic note that he wanted no "cross or any other instrument of torture or symbol of blood sacrifice" to commemorate him.

Shaw came to Ayot St Lawrence with his wife in 1906, after numerous moves from place to place searching for an ideal house where he could live and work in peace but be within easy reach of London (a requirement which has brought many writers and artists to Hertfordshire). Neither G.B.S. nor Charlotte liked the New Rectory especially., and intended to rent it only until they found something better, but a few years after moving in, they bought it, and spent the rest of their lives there. Shaw never really took to the house, but he was getting too old to keep moving, and in any case had a certain indifference to his surroundings which is common among writers. He renamed it Shaw's Corner and left it to the National Trust in his will. Visitors can see the great man's study and his notebooks full of impeccable shorthand writing, and the garden in which his ashes and those of his wife were scattered. Nearly all Shaw's best work was already behind him by the time he came to this village, but here he wrote the play which I, and many critics, regard as his finest, *Heartbreak House*, and the one he himself thought his best, *Back to Methuselah*.

Codicote is not an attractive village today, but its timbered inn, the George and Dragon, built about the middle of the sixteenth century, is on the site of what was probably Hertfordshire's earliest alehouse, licensed before 1279. It stood in front of an open space in the medieval village where the market was held, and it was standing when the Black Death struck, killing eighty-four tenants in the village – a remarkably high number which Codicote nevertheless survived, though the disaster may have had something to do with the fact that the village shifted its centre from its old church to the road between Hitchin and Welwyn.

Here and at Datchworth, on the other side of the A1(M), we can dismiss with confidence Pevsner's suggestion that nowhere in Hertfordshire can you forget the closeness of London. Not only because of the agricultural country and the pleasant woods all around, but also because the villages themselves more readily remind us of the ancient country folklore not long forgotten here. Stories of ghosts, witches, resurrection-men and ancient superstitions abound in these villages. The residents of Codicote, who once found the body of a man dug up from his grave and left in the churchyard because the grave-robber had been disturbed, reverently buried him again and then, no doubt, went into the church to touch the Old Dog of Codicote for good luck – a medieval carving of a grotesque animal with a monkey's head, and undoubtedly a pagan symbol.

Datchworth must be the most haunted village in the county. Whitehorse Lane, Hawkins Hall Lane, Bramfield Lane and Rectory Lane each has its own ghost story, the latter being of a horseless cart which trundles along the lane towards the graveyard, and possibly derives from the alleged death from starvation and neglect of four people in the poorhouse in the eighteenth century.

At Knebworth House, the only significant ghost is the house itself, a spectre of the Gothic Revival spirited out of an earlier mansion on the site by the Victorian novelist Edward Bulwer-Lytton. The Lytton family and their successors have owned Knebworth since 1492, and the bulk of their monuments – "the most remarkable display of family pride in the county", as Pevsner calls them – are in the church standing in the grounds. Bulwer-Lytton himself, however, who became an M.P., Colonial Secretary and then Baron Lytton of Knebworth, is buried in Westminster Abbey. The fact that Carlyle disapproved of the dandyish Bulwer-Lytton might be considered in the latter's favour, but that Lytton was a man of immense conceit cannot be doubted, and his house seems to me to stand as witness to his egotism. Disraeli once described someone as "the most conceited man I ever met, though I have read Cicero and known Bulwer-Lytton".

Lord Lytton was the link in time between Sir Walter Scott and Charles Dickens, who was often at Knebworth, along with other friends of Lytton's such as Wilkie Collins and the painter Daniel Maclise. Lytton's novels included *The Last Days of Pompeii* and *Rienzi*, which inspired Wagner's opera, but his works are hardly read nowadays and the only words of his which everyone knows occur in his play *Richelieu* – "The pen is mightier than the sword."

It is ironic that the present owner of the family estate, Lord Cobbold, a former Governor of the Bank of England, should have been the last Lord Chamberlain of the Queen's Household to exercise the unenviable duty of censoring the work of the pen when put to the service of the stage – 'a duty which has, at his and others' hands, suppressed the words of important writers from Fielding to John Osborne, and including Bernard Shaw, who described one of Lord Cobbold's predecessors in the office as "a gentleman who robs, insults and suppresses me as irresistibly as if he were the Tsar of Russia . . ." "It is a frightening thing," Shaw wrote, "to see the great thinkers, poets and authors of modern Europe – men like Ibsen, Wagner, Tolstoy and the leaders of our own literature – delivered into the vulgar hands of such a noodle as this amiable old gentleman."

Despite all its literary associations, Knebworth House seems very far away from any serious concern with literature. The park has been turned into a popular pleasure-ground and the house itself has an air about it of the seaside showplace. What remains of the brick-built Jacobean original is swamped *inside* by a claustrophobic Victorian accumulation of trivia, and *outside* by a stucco disguise to justify the mock-Tudor towers, battlements, turrets and gargoyles which Lord Lytton's gardener referred to, with sublime contempt, as "bloody monkeys". One should visit Hatfield House and Knebworth on the same day in order to feel the full impact of the difference between the genuine and the sham.

The places clustered round the A1(M) and, like it, separating Stevenage from Hitchin, include the lost village of Chesfield, which has been in the parish of Graveley since 1445, although in the preceding century the boundaries between the two had been so hotly disputed that the parson of one killed the parson of the other in a territorial dispute, after which Parson's Green nearby was named.

Jack's Hill, a stretch of the former Great North Road above Graveley, was named after a legendary giant called Jack o'Legs, who lived and was buried at Weston, and whose story has remarkable, indeed suspicious, similarities to Robin Hood's. He lived in a cave, was a dab hand with bow and arrows, and robbed the rich to give to the poor, until he was hanged by the local traders whose goods he stole. Weston is a particularly neat and spacious village with friendly ducks on its pond, and it seems to be the centre of an oasis of pasture land in this arable farming country, with fields of sheep all around it.

Ippollitts, or St Ippollitts, as it is more properly called, is deduced by the old historians of the county, on account of their knowledge of Greek, to have taken its name from a third-century horse doctor, though why it should have done so, they do not adequately explain. All the same, gullible farmers were permitted to lead their ailing nags into the parish church, at one time, so that the services of the saint could be called upon to heal the animals, not so much face to face as halter to altar. Little Wymondley, nearby, is considerably larger these days than Great Wymondley, to the north, while to the east of Stevenage, the villages of Benington, Walkern and Ardeley represent the threshold of that north-eastern quarter of Hertfordshire which is the least spoiled part of the county, where Ends and Greens lie dotted among the country lanes and rich farmland, and where major roads are noticeably fewer.

Although Ardeley and Benington have much to recommend them to the notice of the visitor, the former having been the home of the county historian Sir Henry Chauncy, and the latter a particularly attractive village, it is Walkern that lays claim to special attention here, for in this village began the series of events that led to the passing of the Witchcraft Act of 1735, to which I promised to return.

Jane Wenham, of Walkern, was accused of bewitching a sixteen-year-old girl named Ann Thorn who, despite a dislocated knee, it was said, suddenly jumped up, ran half a mile, and leapt over a five-barred gate. Jane Wenham, seventy years old, was ducked in the pond and then brought before the local magistrate, none other than our old friend Chauncy. He ordered four women to search her for the marks of familiar spirits on her body, then committed her for trial at Hertford.

Evidence was given against her by three clergymen and the servants of the local rector. One of the clergymen, the Rev. Francis Bragge, fanatical vicar of Hitchin, published a pamphlet against witches which ran into five editions. He was hardly an impartial witness, and clearly feelings ran high. Another Hitchin man, William Drage, had published a 'medical' work some years before in which he said that anyone may be considered bewitched who vomits "knives, scissors, eggs, dog-tails, crooked nails, pins, needles, live eels . . ." and so on, " . . . or who fly, run up the walls with their feet uppermost," etc.

Well, certainly *something* would be seriously wrong with them, but *witchcraft*? One man who did not believe a word of it was the judge, Mr Justice Powell. For once, the judge was the hero of the affair. For though this was "the age of reason", and the worst excesses of the witch-craze were long since over, it was a case brought by the still ignorant mob, and Mr Justice Powell, whom Swift once described as "the merriest old gentleman I ever saw", had to sit in the court listening to witnesses saying that attempts to draw blood from Jane Wenham's arm by running a pin into it had failed; that she could not say the Lord's Prayer; that she was able to fly . . . "There is," observed the judge splendidly, "no law against flying." He then summed up in a fashion that left no doubt that he expected an acquittal, but Jane Wenham was found guilty, and he had no alternative but to condemn her to death. He took the opportunity to say that "the same Ignorance and Superstition which had instigated her accusers to apprehend her, operated in the minds of twelve men, sworn to do justice; and they, to their eternal shame, found her guilty".

Judge Powell did not let matters rest there, however. He interceded with the Queen on the old woman's behalf, and she was granted a reprieve. She died at Hertingfordbury in 1730, the last person to be condemned to death for witchcraft in England, for her case created the furore which led to the abolition of the death penalty for witches. It was said that the girl Ann Thorn was an idle hussy whose malicious accusations ceased when her sweetheart turned up and married her.

So we come to Hitchin, which has often been described as, next to St Albans, Hertfordshire's most attractive town. On the whole this is still true, but in some respects Hitchin is the county's most attractive town bar none. What its parish church lacks in comparison with St Albans Abbey (and that is only a matter of scale), Hitchin makes up for in other ways. For one thing, unlike St Albans, it does not lie on any major modern trunk road; but in the old coaching days, it was a staging post of great importance, so it has a wealth of old inns with stabling yards, and its streets radiate from the market square which was its medieval centre. Particularly good is the yard of the Red Hart in Bucklersbury, where the smiths and armourers of the town had their workshops.

Hitchin's name has been fancifully identified with the Iceni tribe by some, and perhaps even more fancifully by others with 'Hicca', another of those conjectural Anglo-Saxon chieftains. St Albans grew up on the wealth of its great abbey; Hitchin on the strength of its trade. It was important in the wool trade, and its merchants built there the biggest parish church in the county, which contains the arms of the Staple of Calais. Struck by lightning, felled by an earth tremor, stripped of its riches during the Reformation and the Civil War, it is a solid and spacious-looking church and, though not beautiful, it contains some beautifully carved stonework.

Other by-products of agriculture - malting, brewing and leather - contributed to the town's prosperity, and it remains aloof from heavier industry to this day. A local tanner was brought before the magistrate in the fifteenth century for polluting the river with the waste products of his trade, and leather is still an important product of the town, one company at the old Tannery, off Bancroft, producing among other things fine bookbinding leathers. Hitchin is also famous for roses, the well-known growers Harkness and Company having their grounds on the road out of the town towards Letchworth.

In these narrow streets with their many old timbered and gabled houses walked George Chapman, Shakespeare's contemporary, and translator of Homer's *Iliad* and *Odyssey*. He was probably born here, in Tilehouse Street. He claimed to have undertaken his chief work, which took him thirteen years, at the command of Homer's ghost, which visited him at Hitchin. From these same streets thirty years after his death the townsfolk saw the sky to the south aglow with the Great Fire of London, before the news had travelled this far, and wondered if London had been sacked like Troy.

Because Hitchin was ruled by its merchants and not, like St Albans, by the Church, its spirit of independence made it ripe for the teachings of Nonconformism. The Quakers gained an early hold on the town, and famous preachers such as Bunyan and George Whitefield were heard here, but Hitchin's development during the seventeenth century was arrested by epidemics of bubonic plague, and Queen Street was once called Dead Street because, according to tradition, every inhabitant of the street was killed by the disease. This, together with the town's reliance on agriculture rather than industry, and the disappearance of the stage coaches which brought passing trade, ensured that Hitchin remained a small market town, and in 1801 its population was only a little over 3,000. Then the railway came (in 1848) and Hitchin has grown considerably since, but it still has only half the population and half the noise of St Albans, yet provides better shopping facilities and seems altogether more welcoming. True, as other writers have complained, many of its old buildings have been ruthlessly destroyed in catering for the shopping needs of a fairly wide area, but people today need twentieth-century facilities, and in Hitchin they are provided without total loss of the style and character that make it such an interesting place to see. In the town's small but attractive museum, the implements of the straw-plaiting trade are on display, together with some examples of the kind of work done by the women who earned their livelihood in this way.

Holwell and Ickleford lie above Hitchin where the Icknield Way crosses the county, and at Ickleford we come across a nice piece of irony, for in 1590 a man named Harding, who claimed to be a witch, so frequently failed to cure ailments with his charms and potions that he was sent to prison for fraud. It is a far, far, better thing, I dare say, to be a success in the company of the Devil than a failure in the custody of the fraud squad.

Further along the Icknield Way past Letchworth, Baldock stands at the crossroads of the ancient trackway and the former Great North Road, so it is no surprise to learn that Romans and Saxons were here laying the foundations of this little market town. But its name, according to Salmon, was given it by the Knights Templar who settled here, and called it after Baldach, a city of their order near Babylon, since known as Baghdad, from which they had been expelled by the Saracens. Be that as it may, the modern town grew up on the strength of its malting and brewing trades, as well as on the importance of its position as a staging post, notwithstanding the remarks of Defoe about its roads:

> Here is that famous lane called Baldock Lane, famous for being so unpassable, that the coaches and travellers were obliged to break out of the way even by force, which the people of the country not able to prevent, at length placed gates, and laid their lands open, setting men at the gates to take voluntary toll, which travellers always chose to pay, rather than plunge into sloughs and holes, which no horse could wade through.

Baldock mended its ways and has many old inns to show for it, and at one of them Samuel Pepys fancied the landlady, but "durst not take notice of her, her husband being there". For this detail and all the other great interest of Pepys' life we are indebted, curiously enough, to a man who is buried in

Baldock church – John Smith, who became rector here. Whilst at Cambridge, Smith laboured for three years over six volumes of closely written shorthand which had lain untouched for nearly a century. He ruined his eyesight in deciphering the work, but did not give up until he had presented to the world the immortal *Diary of Samuel Pepys*.

It is at Baldock's church of St Mary where the 'Hertfordshire Spike' comes into its own. Insofar as this apology for a spire, to be seen throughout the county, can be called an architectural style at all, Baldock has a specially good example of it. The recent A1 bypass has given Baldock a well-earned retirement from its career as a bottle-neck. Its centre, with its wide main street, has borne the weight of through-traffic on the Great North Road for centuries, and many a long-distance lorry driver has been misled there by the double turn in the old road.

The villages surrounding Baldock – Clothall, Norton, Radwell and Bygrave – are of interest chiefly for their curious exemption from the agricultural enclosures of the eighteenth century. Bygrave and Clothall, in particular, had open fields which were farmed in strips until after the First World War, and Bygrave has been called "one of the most interesting survivors of a primitive self-contained settlement in England", its farms and houses clustered round the moated manor and church, and its parish boundaries formed by the Icknield Way and the Cat Ditch. Clothall's church, with its rather squat tower, is perched on top of a little hill which causes the road to go off-course round its foot.

In this northern extremity of Hertfordshire beyond Baldock, if we have not completely escaped the influence of London before, we unquestionably escape it now. This is the true Hertfordshire, left in peace by the commuter and by industry, where the effect of the weather on the wheatfields is of more importance in life than the cocktail party or the time of the next train. And if you should doubt that it is possible in this county for any village to seem lonely and remote, make your way to Caldecote, which stands with its tiny church away from any through road. The land in this area is relatively flat and open, devoid of woodland and the enclosed effect of high hedges and tree-lined roads; where the levelling of the ground for arable land was pushed to the limit by the early farmers, and has never been changed. The roads are separated from the fields by ditches rather than hedges, and the district seems to belong to the Cambridgeshire fens rather than to Hertfordshire, except for the undulations in the landscape.

Newnham and Hinxworth are small villages which reinforce this pleasing impression of agricultural continuity, Hinxworth being the most northerly village in the county, but it is at Ashwell, a larger village two miles east, where our attention is suddenly riveted by a place of unexpected interest. It is undeniably, I think, one of Hertfordshire's most fascinating villages.

That Ashwell was an ancient settlement can be easily deduced from its proximity to the Icknield Way and Arbury Banks, an Iron Age hillfort, and from the fact that here is a source of the river from which Cambridge takes its name. That Ashwell was prosperous in the Middle Ages is instantly evident from the size and style of its fourteenth-century church of St Mary the Virgin, spacious and austere, with its magnificent tower, 176 feet high, surmounted by a decorative spike similar to Baldock's. The history of this village is written in its stones, both literally and metaphorically.

In the summer of 1349, the Black Death struck Ashwell, and it seems probable that this village, like Codicote, was hit especially hard, thus putting an end to its economic pre-eminence in the district, which then passed to Baldock, and putting paid to its weekly market as well. The people brought out their dead from the timber-framed houses lining the streets, the crops were left to rot in the fields, and in the following year a literate villager scratched on the wall of the church tower that desperate Latin S.O.S. we noticed in the first chapter: ". . . the dregs of the people alone survive to witness". It has been suggested that one of the masons scratched the words on the stones, as the church was still in course of building at that date. But the masons would probably not have known Latin, and it was more likely a monk who left the message.

Stark and horrible as the inscription is, however, 'survive' is the operative word, and Ashwell was too large to become one of Hertfordshire's lost villages. It progressed and throve on farming, malting, chalk quarrying and straw-plaiting, until disaster struck again, in 1850, when fire raged through the village for twenty-four hours and destroyed farms, cottages, malt-houses and two chapels. It is believed the fire was started deliberately by a disgruntled labourer. But still the village kept going. Its remaining timber-framed and gabled brick houses have been described as some of the best domestic architecture in England, and its newer houses of buff brick clearly indicate the extent of the destruction caused by the fire.

More of the village's past can be seen in its little museum, begun by two schoolboys, which is housed in a Tudor building near the church, originally the Tithe Office of the Abbot of Westminster, who was lord of the manor until the dissolution. Ashwell also preserves its village lock-up, like numerous other places in the county, though why anyone should think these unattractive hovels, in which a person guilty of some misdemeanour was liable to be shut away in total darkness on a bed of straw, worth preserving is quite beyond my understanding. We have a craze for preservation today which makes no distinction between the beautiful, the valuable, the useless and the loathsome.

Ashwell gets its name from the spring, surrounded by ash trees, which is the source of the River Rhee, main tributary of the Cam. The village street still runs, to this day, beside the spot which was the source of Ashwell's foundation. "Goo aan oop theer", an old man said to me, pointing out the way. The water bubbling up through the ground at various points is said to be always at the same temperature, winter and summer alike. Beyond the village and the county boundary, a long green track called Ashwell Street goes to the east, straight as an arrow. It may have been a prehistoric track, or a Roman road, or a medieval drove-road – who knows?

A village where they made saltpetre from pigeons' droppings must have had a community sense of humour, despite its catastrophes, and perhaps the key to Ashwell's survival is to be found among the fourteenth-century graffiti in the church, for though they are in Latin, they are not all equally doomladen, and among the inscriptions on the columns in the nave is one in which we can readily recognize our own kith and kin, and which created a precedent for more recent scrawls of less momentous import than the Black Death inscription: *Barbara filia barbara est.* I wonder if a monk wrote that! We can translate this 'dog-Latin' into the modern English idiom as "Barbara is a bitch."

VII

THE WAY TO THE WASH

THE A10, partly on the course of the Roman Ermine Street, and sometimes called the Great Cambridge Road, is in one respect the worst and in another the best of all the major roads through the county. It leaves Enfield and comes up through a heavily built-up and depressing area, via Waltham Cross and Cheshunt, which gives one no sense of relief at having escaped London and reached Hertfordshire. Halfway through its long course through the county, past Hertford and Ware, it begins to look more promising, and although it is still an important major road, it then passes through that north-eastern part of Hertfordshire where, as we have noticed, agricultural interests still reign supreme, and where the villages and countryside are least affected by London's scorching fallout. It leaves the county at Royston and heads for Cambridge and the sea, and thus has a less overwhelming sense of urgency than the industrial roads to the Midlands and the north. And once past the Hertford/Ware build-up, it is Hertfordshire's safest trunk road, less accidents occurring on it than on any of the others. This is not altogether surprising when one considers the nature of the country it passes through. Much of the land here comes within the rural districts of Hitchin and Braughing – large territories with almost as many acres as people. At the 1971 census, for instance, Hitchin Rural District contained just over 25,000 people in 21,000 acres, compared with Watford's so-called rural district, which had more than twice as many people in a third of the space – over seven persons to the acre against hardly more than one in the Hitchin area.

Waltham Cross is best got through as quickly as possible on its congested main street, for it has nothing to show but its surviving Eleanor Cross, and although this is an interesting piece of Gothic architecture, it is so completely hemmed in by the modern buildings around it that it looks wildly incongruous, and appreciation of its qualities is practically impossible. It would be better taken down and rebuilt in a park or some other less frantic and ugly spot, where the vibration of heavy traffic would not affect it. The cross has already been restored on a number of occasions, most recently after a shaking by the bombs of the Second World War. Anthony Trollope was the most famous resident of Waltham Cross. He lived for twelve years in a house not far from the cross, and wrote some of his best-known novels there, including *The Small House at Allington* and *The Last Chronicle of Barset.*

The dead straight and purposeful railway line through Waltham Cross and Cheshunt neatly separates the built-up area from the River Lea to the east, with the county boundary following a more tipsy course along the river, beyond which is the marshy valley and Essex. To the west, however, just inside the Hertfordshire border with Middlesex, is the site of that Elizabethan mansion, Theobalds, already mentioned in connection with Hatfield.

The road near the site passes the most curious of all Hertfordshire's monuments, Sir Christopher Wren's original Temple Bar. It was built at the top of Fleet Street in 1672, with a huge main gateway flanked by smaller gates for pedestrians. For two hundred years it stood in London, witnessing great events at the heart of the capital, and having the bloody heads of traitors impaled on it, including Lord Lovat's. But inevitably, with the increasing volume of traffic, it became an obstruction, and was dismantled. It was bought by the then owner of Theobalds, Sir Henry Meux, and re-erected here in 1878, where it has remained, an obvious city building befitting the centre of Paris, in a Hertfordshire country lane. There is a move afoot as I write to have the monument restored and returned to a more suitable site in London.

Theobalds is pronounced 'Tibbalds' locally, and the name has survived in subsequent buildings although Lord Burghley's mansion was demolished during the Commonwealth. James I swopped Hatfield Palace for Theobalds because he fancied it as a hunting lodge convenient for Enfield Chase, and it was here where he died, senile and feeble-minded, in 1625, and where Charles I was proclaimed King. As well as hunting the deer, James kept cormorants for fishing, and in the gardens, which Burghley had made among the finest in England, was a maze which John Evelyn tells us was "demolish'd by the rebels". If Cromwell knew the pagan origin of mazes, it is little wonder that, with all its royalist associations as well, he had the place pulled down.

The best story of the old Theobalds is that told us by Sir Francis Bacon, concerning Queen Elizabeth's visit to the house in Lord Burghley's time. The Queen consented to make seven knights before she departed, and Burghley had them lined up in the hall in order of his own choosing, rather than in order of seniority or importance. Bacon continues:

> The Queen was told of it, and said nothing; but when she went along, she passed them all by, as far as the skreen, as if she had forgot; and when she came to the skreen, she seemed to take herself with the manner and said "I had almost forgot what I promised." With that she turned back, and knighted the lowest first, and so upward. Whereupon Mr Stanhope, of the privy-chamber, a while after told her, "Your Majesty was too fine for my Lord Burleigh." She answered, "I have but fulfilled the Scripture, the first shall be last, and the last first."

Cardinal Wolsey and Richard Cromwell lived at Cheshunt, too, as well as a less famous but perhaps more useful man, Jeremiah Grew, a doctor who was an important pioneer in the study of vegetable anatomy. Cromwell came here to live in his old age – under the name of Clarke – with Mrs Pengelly, long after the Restoration, and died here in 1712.

The area between Cheshunt and Cuffley is an important market gardening district with a difference, for the speciality here is growing under glass, and there are acres of greenhouses to be seen all around. Salad crops are the chief products, but other things are grown as well, such as flowers and

Wren's Temple Bar, defended against vandalism

The New River monument to Sir Hugh Myddelton at Great Amwell

Hertford: the castle gatehouse (*above*) and the Bluecoat School

The Great Bed of Ware

(*above*) Derelict gazebos and an old malting by the River Lea at Ware

(*below*) The village green and pump at Westmill

(*facing*) Braughing

(*above*) The church of the lost village of Layston

(*below*) The village street in Much Hadham

(*facing*) Furneaux Pelham

Exercising racehorses on Royston Heath

mushrooms. The well-known specialists in indoor plants, Rochfords, started business at Cheshunt in 1883 with a single greenhouse. Within fifteen years, the family owned 86 acres of glass, and it was thought that, outside Middlesex and Kent, the area under glass in Cheshunt alone was equal to all the rest in England and Wales. More recently, retail trade has become important to Cheshunt, too, as it is the headquarters of Sir John Cohen's 'Tesco' chain of supermarkets.

Broxbourne, stretched out along the old north road, was originally a large parish of which the hamlet of Hoddesdon was a part. Now the roles are reversed, but the old order meant that Broxbourne had a large church, mainly of sixteenth and seventeenth-century work, whereas Hoddesdon's is smaller and modern. Broxbourne church thus contains the memorials to Hoddesdon's long-dead, among whom is John Macadam, the famous Scottish road engineer, who lived in Hoddesdon towards the end of his life, and died only thirteen years after another local man, Edward Christian, whose younger brother Fletcher led the mutiny on the *Bounty*. Macadam employed a Hoddesdon man, George Allen, to make tools for him, among which was a metal ring supplied to road-builders to gauge the stone used for the thick bed of his roads. If a stone would not pass through the ring, it was too large. Allen once asked Macadam what the stone-breaker was to do if he lost the ring. "Why George," Macadam replied, "let him try the pieces in his mouth. If they go in they will be small enough." Now Hoddesdon and the country to the west are to have the North Orbital motorway inflicted on them.

At the eastern edge of Hoddesdon is the remaining gatehouse of the moated Rye House, close to a sewage works and a confusion of waterways where the New River and the Lea Navigation run parallel to the river and the Stort flows into the Lea at the county boundary. The Rye House is somewhat the worse for wear nowadays, having been used as a pleasure centre for many years and then abandoned to the elements and damaged by fire about forty years ago. But it is due for restoration, and it was here where the Rye House Plot was hatched, which might have altered the course of English history by the assassination of Charles II, had it not been discovered in time. It led, instead, to the execution of most of those implicated, but the Earl of Essex (of Cassiobury) was found with his throat cut in the Tower. Richard Rumbold, the alleged ringleader of the conspirators, was captured later and executed at Edinburgh.

The effluent of the Rye Meads Sewage Works, which treats the sewage of Stevenage and Welwyn Garden City, travels down-river to be picked up again as cooling water by the Rye House Power Station, which then discharges it a mile downstream. Industrial activity of this sort has made a largely derelict landscape of the Lea Valley, but a major reclamation scheme is in progress under the Lee Valley Regional Park Authority – a government-sponsored fun committee. Set up by Act of Parliament in 1966, this body has the task of creating a so-called Regional Park along 23 miles of the River Lea (they may spell it their way but I will spell it mine!) to provide leisure activities for the people of North London, Essex and Hertfordshire.

Only a narrow strip of the northern part of this park falls in Hertfordshire, mainly on the east side of the railway through Waltham Cross, Cheshunt and Hoddesdon, until it turns north-west from the Rye House area to surround Stanstead Abbots and reach the southern outskirts of Ware. Its effect on the county, however, will be enormous. Major watersports facilities will be a prominent feature of the Hertfordshire parts of the park, particularly between Ware and Stanstead Abbots, and a new dual carriageway Park Road is to be built from the A10 near Amwell Hill to run right through the area, with a maximum capacity of 3,200 vehicles per hour in each direction. "The development of the Park itself," the Authority concedes, "must inevitably increase the volume of traffic using roads in the valley. . . ." Over two million people, it says, will live within half an hour's car journey of the park.

By 1984, the Regional Park will be a reality, and to the tyranny of television we shall have to add the tyranny of slide-rule leisure planning: one more step on the road to changing "doing your own thing" to doing the government's thing. The recovery and landscaping of waste-land is to be heartily applauded, of course, but other implications of the undertaking are less heartening, leading the conditioned populace of the future, I suspect, to imagine it lives in an earthly paradise which is really only a conveyor belt with coloured lights, travelling from cradle to grave.

Let us turn hastily back to the Lea of earlier days, for it is specially associated with a man who died in the year of the Rye House Plot, but seemed of a different world from that event – the admirable Izaak Walton. His famous work *The Compleat Angler* is a sort of walking commentary on a five-day angling holiday spent in travelling from Tottenham to the river around Hoddesdon, Ware and Amwell, and then back again after fascinating discussions about fish, otters, rivers and other country interests. Walton's masterpiece, which as Charles Lamb said "breathes the very spirit of innocence, purity and simplicity of heart", has long been recognized as one of the most delightful books in the English language, and among the particular places he mentioned is the Thatched House inn at Hoddesdon, where he was inclined to go for his morning cup of ale. Alas, the Thatched House was long ago demolished, to be followed by the Maidenhead and the Bull, but other old inns survive at Hoddesdon, where we are entering the domain of another occupation centred in the valley of the Lea, Hertfordshire's traditional malting industry, but of that we will treat more fully when we come to Ware.

Meanwhile, the villages on the south and east sides of the county capital beckon for our attention, and on the high ground to the west of the Lea valley we find Bayford, with pleasant views and the Baker Arms, which has nothing to do with bread but is named after the builder of Bayfordbury, the large house a mile away. It was built around 1760 by Sir William Baker, whose most amiable action was his refusal of a baronetcy, on the grounds that the lesser honour of knighthood would "confine the folly to himself and entail no ridicule on his descendants".

No such sensible scruple troubled the first Earl Cowper, though his family came very close to bringing ridicule on his descendants. Earl Cowper himself was a none-too-popular Lord Chancellor, and his brother, a lawyer, was sent to trial for the murder of a Quaker woman who was found floating in the river after Cowper had visited her home. The judge in the case was unable to sum up because he felt faint and had forgotten the evidence, but instead of having a retrial, Cowper was acquitted and later became a judge himself. Faith and Justice stand either side of him on his monument by Roubiliac in Hertingfordbury church, which also contains a tablet to the Lord Chancellor's mistress as well as other monuments to the Cowper family. The church was practically rebuilt by the seventh Earl, but it contains some impressive oak bench-ends carved by Joseph Mayer of Oberammergau.

The seat of the Cowpers was Panshanger, now demolished, which was known for, among other things, a famous oak tree in its garden. The Panshanger Oak was described by Gilbert White, the eighteenth-century naturalist, as being probably "the finest and most stately oak now growing in the south-east of England". It was the subject of a Tree Preservation Order in 1953. From the road on the north side of the estate, between Hertford and Tewin, there is a pleasing view of the Mimram meandering through the meadows.

From Amwell Hill, Izaak Walton and his friends could look down on meadows "chequered with water-lilies and lady-smocks". But already, when Walton was here, and when men plotted nearby to kill the King, Great Amwell was famous for its New River, an artificial waterway constructed in 1613 to carry much-needed water to London. It was the work of Sir Hugh Myddelton, a wealthy mine-owner, alderman and Member of Parliament, who proposed the idea to the Corporation and was authorized by Act of Parliament to carry it out (at his own expense!), to bring water from springs at Chadwell and Great Amwell "by means of a trench of the breadth of ten feet and not above". The Corporation was to make and maintain convenient bridges and ways "for the passage of the King's subjects over the said river or cut". The oldest bridge still in use is an iron one built in 1824 to carry a byroad across the New River from the A10 south of Ware to Great Amwell village, where an island in the river has a monument to Myddelton set among weeping willows in one of the county's most attractive spots. The original channel carried the water from the springs 40 miles to Clerkenwell, but it was subsequently shortened, and then water from the Lea was fed into it (at the rate of more than twenty million gallons a day in modern times), when the Chadwell spring was thought to be drying up. New River Company shares were worth a fortune in the nineteenth century. The Metropolitan Water Board took over its operations in 1904.

The road through Little Amwell and Hertford Heath is on the course of the original Ermine Street for a short distance, where it is called Elbow Lane, and was obviously well known to one Phillipe Winchley, "an owlde notorius bedlam roge", who earned himself a mention in the parish records by dropping dead in a field "as hee travelled along". The road takes a sharp turn into Hertford at this point, after passing Haileybury College. This is a building of classical design, fronted by a six-column portico, and was built as a training college for the East India Company in 1809, and later became a public school. Among its later pupils were Edmund Allenby – Field Marshal Viscount Allenby whose brilliant campaign defeated the Turkish army in the First World War – and Clement Attlee, who became Prime Minister after the Second World War. But during its East India Company days, it was a teacher rather than a pupil who brought distinction to Haileybury. The Rev. Thomas Malthus was appointed Professor of History and Political Economy there, when he was already famous as the author of a theory of population which influenced Darwin and is still a matter of controversy; advancing the proposition that without birth control, the world's population will always increase faster than the means of subsistence.

Stanstead Abbots, across the river, is notable for the attractive eighteenth-century interior of the hilltop village church of St James, which contains among its memorials one to Sir Felix Booth. But it is not the only memorial to this member of a family of distillers. If you look at a map of Canada, inside the Arctic Circle between Baffin Island and Victoria Island you will find the Gulf of Boothia and the Boothia Peninsula, and not far away is the North Magnetic Pole. Booth never travelled so far himself, but he financed one who did, the polar explorer Sir James Clark Ross, who discovered the Magnetic Pole while seeking the North West Passage. His ship *Endeavour* was fitted out by Felix Booth entirely at his own expense, and the King made Booth a baronet for his generous contribution to science, but Ross, in naming various points on his voyage after the man who made the expedition possible, gave him more lasting and rewarding recognition.

Meanwhile, our own exploration has brought us, at last, to the discovery of the county capital. The market town of Hertford grew up around the fortified townships founded here by Edward the Elder to defend Wessex against the Danelaw, at a strategic point where the Rivers Mimram, Rib and Beane join the Lea. It was the chief town of the shire by the tenth century, in spite of the ancient ecclesiastical importance of St Albans. Yet Hertford is a puzzling town – attractive in parts; smaller than one would expect (its population is considerably smaller than those of St Albans and Hitchin, to say nothing of Watford and Stevenage); and above all, a strange and unsatisfactory combination of ancient and modern.

The fate of Hertford's parish churches is symptomatic of the little town's feverish appearance, for there were five in medieval times, but all of them have been lost, three having disappeared entirely and the other two rebuilt in modern times with virtually no trace of ancient beginnings. Those which disappeared included the parish churches of the two original townships, or burhs, on opposite sides of the river – St Mary on the north bank and St Nicholas on the south. The church of St Andrew was rebuilt in 1869 by Earl Cowper, and its only architectural distinction is its untypical broach spire. This was built as an afterthought in 1876, and fifteen years later the ancient church of All Saints was burnt down, and rebuilt in a red stone which makes this, too, rare in the county and not altogether fitting. It is the Friends' Meeting House, built in 1669 in what is now Railway Street (more's the pity), which emerges as Hertford's most interesting place of worship. It is said to be the oldest Quaker meeting house still in use in the world. It is worth repeating that Hertfordshire has been, and still is, an area of fairly strong Quaker influence. William Penn made many converts in the south-west, and George Fox mentions, in his journal, a visit to Hertford in 1655, "where there were some convinced, and where there is now a fine meeting".

Hertford Castle is hardly more rewarding than its churches. Only a few walls and a rebuilt brick gatehouse remain, although their position beside the Lea is still attractive. William the Conqueror built the first improvement on Edward's castle here and it became a place of some importance to English and foreign monarchs, who saw it – according to their different persuasions – as a fortress, a prison, a hunting lodge or a country house. It was besieged by the French Dauphin in 1216, and among others, David Bruce of Scotland and John of France were held captive in it. Every English ruler up to Elizabeth I seems to have stayed in it at some time, but Charles I granted it to the second Earl of Salisbury, and what was left of the original castle – the western gatehouse – was rebuilt as a private mansion.

For a brief period in the early nineteenth century, the gatehouse became a college for the East India Company, before it moved to its own premises at Haileybury, and here on one occasion the startled boys were exhorted to go home to their wives and children, by an absent-minded cleric who was apt to re-use sermons he had composed for other occasions.

A hundred years later, the castle gatehouse was leased by the Marquess of Salisbury to the Hertford Corporation for half a crown a year, since when the grounds have been used as a public park. This is entered from a street called The Wash, but the approach is now overwhelmed by the hideous new Civic Hall of the East Hertfordshire District Council, with its roof vaguely like the old malting kilns, and this monstrous building also looms into unwelcome view as one enters Maidenhead Street from Salisbury Square or Bull Plain (the old cattle market). The Wash, so called because the nearby Lea ran into it when it overflowed its banks, leads into Parliament Square, the town centre, and from the square one enters Fore Street, where the Corn Exchange and the great brick Shire Hall flank the entrances to the old triangular market place.

Fore Street leads to the Christ's Hospital School for Girls, built soon after the Friends' Meeting House, and distinguished by its gateway with figures of Bluecoat Boys, made of lead, which have been there since 1721. One boy faces All Saints Church and the other looks towards the former gaol, and the story goes that the figures recall the murder of one schoolboy by another; the villain having been hanged in one building and the victim buried in the other. Little of the original building remains, however, and what Hertford lacks in large old public buildings and churches, it makes up to some extent in its domestic architecture and inns. The oldest surviving inn is the Salisbury Arms, which was called the Bell in coaching days and was in business early in the fifteenth century.

The Corn Exchange seems more symbolic of Hertford than the Shire Hall or the modern County Hall on its hilltop setting. For Hertford has always been a market town of modest size concerned with malting, brewing and corn-milling. McMullen's Brewery is the only one now remaining in the town. Hertford has been saved from the fate of Watford by its situation away from the major road routes out of London, and although the coming of the railway brought some light industry here, the rapid expansion that might well have resulted did not happen. It was probably the building of County Hall in 1939 (in neo-Georgian style with a somewhat ironic Scandinavian influence), that enabled Hertford to maintain its status as the county town in the face of the obvious claims of St Albans, and the less obvious ones of Watford.

Not surprisingly, Hertford has made little mark on the world of arts and sciences. A thinly disguised appearance in

Jane Austen's *Pride and Prejudice* on the one hand, and the birth here of Edmund Gunter and Richard Westall on the other, are as much as it can boast. Gunter was a mathematician who invented various surveying and navigational devices. Richard Westall was Queen Victoria's childhood drawing master, but although he became a Royal Academician, he was hardly more than a competent illustrator.

Possibly of greater significance in both the long and the short run was a nineteenth-century Hertford barber, William Caffyn, who played cricket for Surrey and England. I have not discovered if his late cut was more highly regarded than his short-back-and-sides, but he gave many a batsman a close shave. He once took 16 wickets for 24 runs against an American team during a tour of the States and Canada, but finally emigrated and taught cricket to the natives of his new country – Australia!

Hertford was the home of one of the first English paper mills, that of John Tate mentioned by Wynkyn de Worde in 1495, and later the bell-founder John Briant had his foundry here. He cast many of the bells in Hertfordshire churches, including those at Hatfield, which were first used in 1786 with a complete peal of 5,120 changes called Oxford Treble Bob. Briant was also a clockmaker of note. Also, Hertford (formerly Hartford – hence the county emblem of a stag) gave birth to one Samuel Stone, who died in Hartford, Connecticut, the town he had founded after following the Pilgrim Fathers across the Atlantic to settle in New England.

If non-dissenting Hertfordshire folk continued to look to St Albans as the spiritual centre of the county, Hertford was the place where the law was administered. Until recently, the Assizes were held in the Shire Hall, and close by, where the Corn Exchange now stands, was the County Gaol, which held those who offended against society's rules and awaited just or unjust punishment, from mere drunkards and petty thieves to murderers and witches. "'Im as prigs what isn't 'isn," a local dialect verse said, "when 'e's cotched'll goo t'prison." To 'prig' was to steal, but a sentence for petty theft was no joke in not-so-far-off days, and the human suffering caused by crime over the centuries has been more than doubled by the judges at the assize court. In 1732, for instance, a labourer named Kilby was ordered to be whipped "until his back be bloody" for stealing a tobacco box worth tenpence. Sixty years later, things had not improved. The gaoler was paid five shillings for burning a prisoner in the hand. Before the century was out, Ann Mead was hanged for poisoning one of her employer's children. She was fourteen. It was another forty years before the last public execution took place in Hertford, by which time a woman named Mary Blanchard had had the distressing experience of travelling to her husband's execution in the same coach as the hangman.

These were the people at the opposite end of the social scale from the dukes and earls and barons whose lives were commemorated in their great houses, their good works and their marble monuments. These ordinary people spent their lives working in the towns or in the fields and died with nothing for posterity to remember them by except a gravestone in the churchyard, if they were good, or an entry in the criminal records, if they were not.

Once in a while, however, one of these working-class people managed to get his name in a footnote in the history books, and one such was Jonas Fosbrooke. He was a journeyman carpenter of Ware, and in 1463 he made a bed of carved oak for King Edward IV, who was so delighted with it that he granted Jonas a life pension. The bed was nearly 11 feet square and 7 feet high, and it became the most famous bed in England, the 'Great Bed of Ware' spoken of with awesome respect in the plays of Shakespeare, Jonson and Farquhar, and now on exhibition as a national treasure – one might say a national monument – in the Victoria and Albert Museum.

What induced Fosbrooke to make such a *huge* bed is not at all clear. Neither the King, nor his wife nor his mistresses, was of outsize proportions, and when the carpenter gave the bed to His Majesty for the use of the royal family and their guests, he cannot have meant all of them at once, though the bed is big enough for four couples. Sir Toby Belch, advising Sir Andrew Aguecheek to write as many lies, to impress his rival in love, "as will lie in thy sheet of paper", adds thoughtfully: "although the sheet were big enough for the Bed of Ware". Of course, there are those who say that the bed is of Elizabethan date, but I believe wholeheartedly in Jonas Fosbrooke. Offended by the attempts of people of lowly rank to sleep in the bed in later years, when both he and the King had passed on, and his craftsmanship filled bedrooms in a succession of local inns, Fosbrooke haunted it, pinching and nipping the presumptuous slumberers until they fled, and thus left his mark on posterity's buttocks as well as his name in its books.

The recently opened Ware bypass weaves its way between Ware and Hertford across King's Meads and relieves the centre of Ware of the heavy A10 traffic which it has had to tolerate for many years. Defoe tells us that an Act of Parliament was obtained

> about 30 years since, for repairing the road between Ware and Royston, and a turnpike was erected for it at Wade's-mill, a village so called, about a mile and a half beyond Ware . . . And, though this road is continuously worked upon, by the vast number of carriages, bringing malt and barley to Ware, for whose sake, indeed, it was obtained; yet, with small repairs it is maintained, and the toll is reduced from a penny, to a half-penny, for the ease of the country, and so in proportion.

This stretch of Ermine Street, the first turnpike road in the country, was essential to the continuing prosperity of Ware as the most important malting town in England, and its significance can be judged from the fact that the county capital was commonly called Hertford-by-Ware at one time. No other town in Hertfordshire can boast such an unbroken industrial tradition as Ware, for maltings were in operation here when William the Conqueror landed on our shores, and it is high time we took a closer look at this industry so important to the Lea and Stort valleys.

Malting is the process by which barley is converted into

malt for the brewing of ale or beer. In the centuries-old method of malting for which all the old Hertfordshire maltings were built, the barley grain was first cleaned and then soaked in water for two or three days. Then the grain, swollen with its increased moisture content, was exposed to air at a constant temperature, spread out over malting floors for one or two weeks, during which germination took place. Finally, when germination had proceeded to the correct stage, the grain was slowly roasted in kilns to produce the malt, and after cooling, and removal of the rootlets, it was ready for delivery to the breweries. Control of the drying process in the kilns varied the colour and flavour of the malt according to its requirements for pale ale, brown ale or stout, and conversion of ale into beer was made in the breweries by the addition of hops. The modern process of malting is similar in principle, but it has been refined by 'drum' malting instead of spreading the grain on floors, and by air conditioning and electrical heating. Many of the old maltings can be seen in this area, though mostly converted to other uses. They are recognizable by their long rows of windows along the shallow floors on two storeys, and by the cowled tops of their kilns.

Ware cannot have suffered temperance workers gladly, for almost the entire population must have been employed in malting or its offshoots at one time, and because of this, its corn market, and its important position on the Great Cambridge Road, it had a huge number of inns for its size, with recognizably old names like the Angel, the Star and the Maidenhead. (All the Ware lads who were not taken in to the maltings must have been employed as ostlers.) Although it is not among the oldest, one of Ware's most interesting inns is the French Horn in High Street. It looks modern, but it is a Jacobean building and was converted to an inn only in the eighteenth century, when touring players gave performances in its assembly room; and one John Clemenson carved his name and the date on a beam in the stables, and then hanged himself from it!

Ware's High Street runs parallel with the Lea, and many of the houses with long gardens running down to the river bank were once graced by gazebos. It is a tragedy that most of them have disappeared, and the few that remain are derelict. They epitomize the startling lack of self-respect that has made Ware so sadly dilapidated now. It is not difficult to imagine what it was like once. Its High Street shops are still alternated with entrances to the stabling yards of the old coaching inns, and its old maltings, yards and narrow streets give it, even now, a character unique in the county. Perhaps the new bypass will help to avoid further demolition of what Hoskins has described as "one of the historic town centres of England".

Between Hertford and Ware there has always been a rivalry which began after the Conquest when Ware's affairs were controlled – to its disadvantage – by the Bailiff of Hertford. Ware retaliated by holding illegal markets on the same days as Hertford's, and by creating weirs in the Lea so that barges could not sail up-river to the county town. An old Hertfordshire saying in these parts has it that "Ware and Wadesmill are worth all London", and this typical local pun is what passes for wit in the county, 'Ware' being meant in the sense of 'merchandise'.

As for Wadesmill, it too is famous for malting. It still has its Feathers, however. There was stabling for "upwards of a hundred horses" at this large village inn, according to Cussans, which must have been a blessing to travellers at Christmas in 1836, when massive snowdrifts of 20 feet, after two days of continuous heavy snow, held up all transport for a week. Wade's mill, on the River Rib, was part of the parish of Thundridge, and the village grew up and took its name from the mill whilst Thundridge itself moved to the main road from its original site further east, where the tower of its former church can still be found.

Further north on the west of the road, the parishes of Great and Little Munden embrace scattered hamlets in this open countryside, the villages themselves having shrunk to such diminutive proportions that they can scarcely be found on the maps. Their respective churches stand as witnesses to justify their names. Great Munden, once called Much Munden, had over a hundred inhabitants when Domesday Book was compiled, but now Little Munden is, if anything, the larger of the two.

I sat near the church of Great Munden one winter's day, beside the foundations of some demolished building, to eat my lunch, and saw no other living thing but a robin which exercised its characteristic curiosity by perching on the wing mirror of my car. I could hear the distant sound of a chain-saw, probably felling a diseased elm. Directly opposite the church, a sign pointed out a public footpath to Herringworth Hall, but as it was straight across the middle of a soggy ploughed field, I resisted the temptation to explore and left it for someone else's book. The hamlet nearest Great Munden is called Nasty, but it is really quite nice, and the place-name experts tell us that the name means "by the east enclosure".

A Roman road, still traceable in parts, ran across this countryside from Baldock to Ermine Street at the point where Standon, Puckeridge and Braughing spread out along road and river. The legions which marched this way have long been forgotten, but a more recent Latin conqueror has not, for it was at Green End, well to the south in Standon's large parish, that villagers fled in panic in September 1784 from the Devil himself coming out of the sky. When a young woman named Elizabeth Brett plucked up courage to hold the rope the visitor had thrown down from his monstrous chariot, the men at last came to help, and the Devil turned out to be Vincenzo Lunardi, Secretary to the Neapolitan Ambassador in London. He was completing the first balloon flight in England, having taken off at Finsbury over two hours earlier.

Standon is an interesting if not a specially attractive village, which is known to have suffered severely during the Black Death, but survived and grew to be the busy little place it is now. It has a former paper mill on the river bank, near what is humorously described as a 'ford'. You may take your car along Paper Mill Lane, through the level crossing gates of the former railway, and down to the water's edge, but there you must stop. (You can take a car to the water but you can't make it swim – new Hertfordshire proverb!)

The children of this village go to school in a splendid old

red brick and timber building dating from the sixteenth century, called the John de Clare primary school. Standon's chief pride, however, is its church, built on a slope, so that steps lead up from nave to chancel, past a superbly carved chancel arch. The church is unique in Hertfordshire in having a tower detached from the main body of the building. John Field, a merchant to whom there is a brass here, lent £2,000 to Henry VIII for the defence of Calais. A God-fearing man of orthodox views, no doubt, he probably bought his meat here, all unwittingly, from one of the county's early heretics, a butcher who was called to account for his belief that there is no god but the sun and moon. The chief monument in this church, however, is to Sir Ralph Sadleir, a Tudor diplomat who built the original mansion known as the Lordship, south of the village. He was said to be the richest commoner in England when he entertained Elizabeth I here.

In the following century, Puckeridge entertained Samuel Pepys during a journey to Cambridge. Staying at the Falcon Inn (now the Crown and Falcon), he was suffering so much in a pair of stiff new shoes that he gave the landlord four shillings for one of his old pairs.

No railway came this way then, and none comes now, but the course of the branch line that served the area until the Beeching axe lopped it off took travellers past the sites of a Belgic settlement and a Roman town near the very attractive village of Braughing (pronounced Braffing). It has been variously spelt Breahingas, Brakinghe and Brawghing over the centuries, but doubtless takes its name from some Saxon upon whose name we will refrain from speculating, except to remark that we could elevate these Saxon noblemen into articles of faith for the place-name experts – "I believe in Wata, Tida and Breahinga . . ." The village has probably evolved from the most important Roman site in Hertfordshire next to Verulamium. It would not be surprising to learn that a considerable town stood near the junction of important routes here, and what has so far been unearthed leaves one to suppose a great deal more remains hidden beneath the surface of what may have been called Curcinati.

Braughing is reached via another of the many fords over the River Rib, this one being passable when the village ducks are not standing in it. Malting Lane gives us the clue to part of Braughing's story, but the church of St Mary tells us much more, for it is an ambitious building compared with most in the area. Part of the nave has a richly decorated roof with two angels, and figures carved in wood and stone look down from the old walls, while Augustin Steward, in alabaster and wearing his immaculate ruff, gazes forward rather starchily.

The gargoyles which look down from the church tower upon the roofs of the lovely old houses surrounding it, as if they could see through the thatch and tiles, were described by Arthur Mee as "grinning". They appear to me, however, to be rather shocked by the life they see going on beneath them, and not altogether without reason. One of the old timbered cottages was once used by the poor newly-weds of the village for their receptions, and it had one room specially reserved for the bridal bed. Then again, one of the best-remembered inhabitants of Braughing was one Matthew Wall, a sixteenth-century farmer, whose body was being taken for burial in the churchyard when the coffin was dropped and the corpse woke up. Banging on the coffin lid brought his recovery to the notice of the startled bearers, and farmer Wall lived on for many more years. It is not *his* ghost that haunts Braughing, however, but those of five monks, who are supposed to walk once every five years as penance for eating fish which they had caught in the river without permission.

There are few signs of art outside the churches in the area, but the modern inn sign of the Adam and Eve is a rewarding thing to come upon in this fertile country. I cannot help wondering if the landlord there sells a lot of cider.

Further up the A10, also beside the Rib, is Westmill, in its own little valley – an exceedingly attractive village whose one-time curate was the misfit Rev. Nathaniel Salmon. Its cottages are ranged round the triangular village green which still sports the old pump, and the village inn, the Sword in Hand, is next door to the church – a convenient arrangement for those who praise the Lord and drink to the Devil.

Delightful as this village is, however, we cannot find excuses to linger here, for the hamlet of Cherry Green, a mile to the west, compels our attention. Here is another of those many connections which Charles Lamb had – "sprinkled about in Hertfordshire" as he put it.

It is the tiny and charming thatched cottage called Button Snap, the only property Lamb ever owned, as he proudly tells us with tongue in cheek:

> When I journeyed down to take possession, and planted foot on my own ground, the stately habits of the donor descended upon me, and I strode (shall I confess the vanity?) with larger paces over my allotment of three quarters of an acre, with its commodious mansion in the midst, with the feeling of an English freeholder that all betwixt sky and centre was my own.

He never lived there, however, and after three years of ownership, sold it to a Mr Greg for £50. I wonder if Lamb knew that in Edward the Confessor's time, the manor in which it stood was owned by a nobleman's servant whose name was Sexi! Nowadays, the cottage is owned by the more respectably sounding Charles Lamb Society, which acquired it from the Royal Society of Arts.

Further down the lane beside the farm is the site of a deserted village called Wakeley. It was never a large settlement, and even before the Black Death it was reported to be half-desolate. No doubt the plague finished the village off, such inhabitants as were left moving elsewhere. The farmer pointed out to me the line of the Roman road which forms the boundary of his property across the fields, while the uneven ground near the farmhouse makes this one of Hertfordshire's more easily traceable lost villages. Often in this county, where lack of building stone meant that houses were built of timber, all signs of building have disappeared under the plough, and the medieval streets and walls can only be traced by excavation, or by the crop marks shown up in aerial photographs. There are large areas of land in this part of the county which, even now, appear sparsely inhabited, and a considerable number of villages are known to have existed once, in Hertfordshire's north-east quarter, which are not there now. Wakeley is typical of them – nothing but a single farm, where in medieval days there were streets and houses with their own little church. The chronicles of St Albans Abbey, which owned much of the land, refer to a cattle pestilence which raged for thirty years at the end of the thirteenth century, and it is probable that this epidemic took away the villagers' livelihood. There is no longer a direct road connecting Wakeley with Westmill, or with Aspenden or Ardeley, and the Roman road nearby is no more than a green tree-lined track across this empty agricultural land. Almost like a desert, with relatively little woodland and few inhabitants, the area seems a world away from the central and western parts of Hertfordshire. Hatfield and Stevenage – let alone Watford and London – seem so remote as to be across the seas, and the London commuter has scarcely penetrated this fine arable land where the edges of the fields support haystacks with their strange wet-and-dry smell; and such small woods as there are have curiosity-arousing names like Beggarman's Wood, Witnesses Wood, and Customs Wood. For my part, I feel as if I am writing a different book from the one I started six chapters ago.

The road through Aspenden comes to nothing, where at one time there must have been a lane to Berkeden, another deserted village, where perhaps the farmers supplied milk to the cheesemaker who is known to have lived at Wakeley. Berkeden, of which there is now no trace at all, was a larger village than Wakeley at the time of the Norman Conquest. Aspenden itself has spread out along the road towards Ermine Street, leaving its church standing rather alone. It was to a private school in Aspenden, run by a clergyman, Rev. Matthew Preston, that Thomas Babington Macaulay came when he was fourteen, to add Greek and Latin to his already prodigious knowledge before proceeding to Cambridge.

The parish of Cottered contains a building, Broadfield Hall, now isolated a mile away from the village, which was once in a separate community of its own with a little church, and all around the district one can find lanes that lead nowhere, ending in a ploughed field or a meadow. Broadfield Hall was once the home of the Forrester family, and one of its daughters married Henry Chauncy. Cottered itself lived through the devastation that emptied so much of this countryside. Its church was standing here when the Black Death deprived the village of a third of its population, but those who were left carried on, and the gabled Lordship house, surrounded by a moat, was built not long afterwards. It is said to be one of Hertfordshire's oldest surviving houses. The church in this lovely old village contains a medieval mural of St Christopher with an interesting landscape background, and a memorial to Sir James Cantlie, who died here and is buried in the churchyard. He was a Scottish surgeon who spent many years in India and China, and was the founder of the Royal Society of Tropical Medicine. The memorial to him was set up by the Chinese government of the time, in this village church which has the unusual Hertfordshire distinction of a spire.

Rushden and Throcking have both left their churches slightly lonely in the course of time, by partial migration or shrinkage. Throcking's is reckoned to be the highest-standing church in the county on its hilltop site. It certainly commands impressive views of the seemingly endless farmland all around it. It is a tiny church, but it contains a good neo-classical marble memorial by Nollekens, erected by the lord of the manor to his wife Hester Elwes, who died in 1770 aged forty-seven. She is represented reading, and we are told that: "In the elegance of her Figure, in the sweetness and civility of her Manners, in the excellence and improvement of her mind and understanding, she excelled the Generality of her Sex." Another curiosity of this church is the carving on one of the choir stalls, which shows three acrobats, one balancing another upside-down on his head, and swinging the third by his leg. A goose has also got into the act, for what reason I am not sure. According to Chauncy, one lord of the manor paved his kitchen with gravestones from the churchyard, and the parish records relate that no marriage, burial or christening took place in the village during two periods of twelve months in the seventeenth century.

To the east of Throcking is a church built in the thirteenth century and dedicated to St Bartholomew, which provides us with an important clue to the reasons for so many villages in this part of Hertfordshire being lost or reduced in size. For this is the church of Layston, but it stands isolated and derelict – a mere shell, with no glass in its stone windows and no roof over its nave. It is surrounded by illegible headstones, and the birds are its only congregation. Some authorities identify Layston with the medieval village named Ichetone. There were probably a hundred people living here who came to church along the treelined path which is now a muddy lane to nowhere. But this village was not wiped out by the Black Death. Most of the church was built after that catastrophe. The answer to its gradual desertion is to be found in the growth of Buntingford along the busy Ermine Street to the west.

A community started to accumulate along the highway in the thirteenth century, where the road is crossed by the river and joined by the road to Baldock. The trade presented by the increasingly busy route brought rapid growth, and in the seventeenth century a chapel-of-ease was built for the people for whom the parish church at Layston was too far away. It was not long before Buntingford was the parish headquarters of a wide area, responsible for the preservation of law and order, and in 1786 one Elizabeth Matthewson of Barkway was "whipped upon her naked body" there, for some unspecified crime. Meanwhile the better standard of living enjoyed by the people of Buntingford naturally attracted those at Layston. Perhaps only the younger people moved away, but as the old died, and no births occurred there, Layston gradually became deserted, its derelict houses crumbled or were pulled down, and its church fell into ruin.

Buntingford throve, and it is now a busy little town – rather too busy, perhaps, for its qualities to be appreciated, with heavy traffic rumbling through its streets tending to deter all thoughts of fine architecture and rustic survivals. But Buntingford preserves its village pump, and nearby are the almshouses founded by Seth Ward, born at Aspenden and educated here, to become in due course Professor of Astronomy at Oxford, Bishop of Exeter, then Bishop of Salisbury, and President of the Royal Society. Pevsner says – and who will doubt him? – that these almshouses are the stateliest in the county.

Buntingford has a Station Road but no station, and one wonders whether the fate that overtook Layston may not yet strike its successor, for there is no law of man or nature which says that villages could only disappear in the Middle Ages, and I have a suspicion that the immense changes being brought about by what we are pleased to call civilization may lead in time to the abandonment of many other communities. Indeed, we are on the way up the A10 to two which have come perilously close to being lost even as I write this book.

Beyond Wyddial and Hare Street ('Hereweye', i.e. army way) lie the villages of Anstey and Nuthampstead, the latter being close to the point where Hertfordshire, Cambridgeshire and Essex meet. Anstey had a motte-and-bailey castle in Norman times. It seems that the castle was demolished in order to build the church with the materials. The church stands close to the remaining castle mound and has, attached to its lychgate, a village lock-up which was at first, according to the *Hertfordshire Mercury* in 1831, so securely constructed that "a few nights ago Thomas Edwards, a man confined therein for disorderly conduct in a public house, effected his escape by pushing one side of the building down". The report is dated 27 December. Tom Edwards obviously got drunk at Christmas and was soon rearrested and jailed again. But what happened to Blind George, an old fiddler who took his dog into a cavern at Cave Gate, to the west of the village? Legend says that the dog emerged trembling with terror and without a hair on its body, but that its master never emerged at all. The cavern, closed up now, is thought to have been a prehistoric flint mine.

The story has an oddly prophetic significance today, for Anstey itself has been in danger of burial. On the east side of Nuthampstead there used to be an R.A.F. airfield from which, during the war, American 'Flying Fortresses' took off on daylight raids. One of them crashed on the mound of Anstey Castle, and its load of bombs sank in the soft mud at the bottom of the moat. After the war, when the base was in R.A.F. use, the official view stated with unconscious irony that the airfield "enlivens the social life of the surrounding villages". Now the land has mostly been reclaimed for agricultural use, but the Commission on the Third London Airport proposed Nuthampstead as a possible site for the development of the major airport needed to supplement Heathrow and Gatwick. A vigorous local campaign was mounted to oppose any such move, and at last succeeded. The development would have meant adding Anstey and Nuthampstead to the list of Hertfordshire's lost villages. A local farmer whose family have been working this land for generations said: "Forty of my ancestors lie in that churchyard. If they are put under concrete, how will they get out on the Day of Judgement?"

Barkway, Reed and Barley sound like a firm of solicitors, but are actually a group of villages on the east side of the A10 in the north-eastern extremity of the county - quiet agricultural communities, each with its own church. There are splendid views of the surrounding countryside from near Reed. This village once had an ancient castle site called Periwinkle Hill, which has now been ploughed almost level, and there are numerous moats in the area which protected early homesteads.

In spite of the fact that Barley's name has nothing to do with the corn grown in its fields (it means 'burial clearing'), the village had an inn called the Old Pharaoh, at the beginning of the eighteenth century, famous for a powerful malt liquor of the same name. It was whimsically maintained that Old Pharaoh, like the King of Egypt, would not let the people go!

Across the Ermine Street again, via Buckland, which need not detain us, we come to Wallington on the road towards Baldock. At first sight we may find nothing of interest to delay us in this village either, but in fact it has played a significant role in modern English literature. The clue is provided by *Kelly's Hertfordshire Directory* for 1937 which lists, under Wallington, "Eric A. Blair, Shopkeeper". Mr Blair was none other than George Orwell, the author of *1984* and *Animal Farm*. He came to this village early in 1936, renting a cottage for 7s. 6d. a week. A year before, it had been the village general store, and Orwell planned to reopen it as such to supplement his meagre income from writing – or, at any rate, to pay his rent. He would write in the mornings and open the shop in the afternoons. Both cottage and garden were in a dreadful state. There was no hot water; the kitchen was liable to be flooded after heavy rain; the cesspool clogged up if thick toilet paper was used. But Orwell was no stranger to rough living and he pressed on, gradually getting the garden in some order, acquiring a goat called Muriel, and writing *The Road to Wigan Pier*, based on his then recent experiences in the north among the unemployed.

Meanwhile, in the village church in June 1936, he married his first wife, Eileen O'Shaughnessy. He wrote to a friend: "I expect we shall rub along all right – as to money I mean – but it will always be hand to mouth as I don't see myself ever writing a best-seller." At the end of the year he went to Spain to fight against the Fascists in the civil war, but was back in the summer of 1937, having narrowly escaped death when a bullet passed straight through his neck. He settled down at Wallington to write his book *Homage to Catalonia*, and grew vegetables and bred hens and ducks, but he gradually became ill with a tubercular lesion in a lung, and had to go into a sanatorium in Kent and then spend a winter convalescing in North Africa. Returning to Wallington once more, he prepared his book of essays *Inside the Whale* for publication, and at the outbreak of war in 1939 tried to get into the army, but was, of course, medically unfit.

Orwell left Wallington in May 1940 and joined the BBC, but he kept the cottage until 1947, renting it out for a time and visiting it on odd occasions when he could. It was in 1943 that he began to write the unforeseen masterpiece *Animal Farm*, and Wallington can claim some contribution to that satirical classic, for just down the road from the cottage, near the church where he was married, is Manor Farm. It gave its name to the most famous farm in modern literature, where the animals take over and evolve their revolutionary maxim, which has passed into the language as the definitive comment on the Stalinist dictatorship: "All animals are equal, but some animals are more equal than others."

Sandon, Kelshall and Therfield are villages where the ancient custom of 'maying' was observed on May Day well into the second half of the nineteenth century. Groups of men dressed in top hats with ribbons hanging down their backs toured the villages leaving May blossom at the door of each house, singing the traditional Mayers' song and collecting gifts. It was the great spring festival, surviving from pre-Roman rituals, the last vestiges of which are to be seen in children dancing round maypoles. These villages, spread along a crest of the Chilterns, are surrounded by hilltops, one of which, near Kelshall, is the site of a Roman burial ground. It is still called Deadman's Hill. Therfield Heath leads on to Royston, the most northerly Hertfordshire town, where Ermine Street crosses the ancient Icknield Way.

Royston is not mentioned in Domesday Book, although one would expect a crossing of such important routes to have had a settlement of some kind in Roman times, and indeed, on the heath (properly called Therfield Heath but more commonly known as Royston Heath) there are five Bronze Age burial mounds and one Neolithic – the latter being the only long barrow in the county. Yet firm evidence of such settlement has not been found, and the origin of Royston is usually ascribed to the Norman period. An Augustinian monastery was founded there in the twelfth century.

In 1742, some workmen in the market place discovered the entrance to a cave, about 28 feet deep, cut out of the solid chalk below the ground. It contained the skeleton of a woman and many crude reliefs carved on the walls. The purpose of the cave and its date have never been satisfactorily explained. The carvings, of religious and legendary figures, have sometimes been attributed to Anglo-Saxon date, but that is regarded as fanciful now, and they are thought more likely to be of late medieval origin. The cave was, at any rate, soon being advertised as "the greatest curiosity of the kind in Europe". It is now maintained by the local council, and is opened to the public on certain days during the summer.

Royston was an important staging post on the old North Road, and the heath a favourite resort of highwaymen. The high ground made this stretch of the road particularly susceptible to winter weather. In 1799 there was a snowstorm of such severity that the York and Wisbech Mail coaches were stuck fast, and in 1836 an even worse one in which the Edinburgh, Boston and Stamford coaches were all stranded in the vicinity, and no mail coach passed through Royston for a week.

The chief interest of the windswept heath was for its sporting activity. King James I had built himself a hunting lodge at Royston, and eventually made it his chief country residence (it was there that he signed the death warrant of Sir Walter Raleigh). The King esteemed the heath, it was said, "beyond all places for ye hunting of ye hare, and yt ye hares here were more stoute and ye sents lay better than in any other places". Naturally, therefore, Royston Heath became a popular centre of hare-coursing in later days, when Cambridge undergraduates and others made themselves nuisances to the local farmers. An announcement in the *Cambridge Chronicle* before the harvest in 1787 said: "We poor farmers round Royston do most humbly beg the favor of the Cambridge gunners, coursers and poachers to let us get home our crops . . ."

The heath is also a favourite haunt of the hooded crow, but the animals most closely associated with the high ground here were not crows, hares or hounds, but horses. King James established races on the heath, and to this day it is used for exercising racehorses. The northern half of Royston was in Cambridgeshire until 1897, and it is hardly more than twenty miles from Newmarket. But it is not only the racehorse breed that is associated with Royston. An old local proverb says: "A Royston horse and a Cambridge Master of Arts give way to no one." The horses referred to were the forerunners of the great Midland shire horses - the draught animals used to pull the malt wagons to London and the carts loaded with corn to Royston market; and the analogy derives from the horses' inviolable right to the road as clearly as that of the University dons' to the pavements of Cambridge.

As for the heath, you have to be there at dawn to experience the exciting atmosphere of rapidly thudding thoroughbred hooves on the springy turf through the early autumn mist - and to feel that all this has precious little to do with Hertfordshire, which is left behind as the A10 passes beyond Royston's built-up area. Let us turn our attention from horses to the cows in yonder fields.

VIII

THE MILKY WAY

WHEN THE M11 MOTORWAY is built from London to Cambridge, it will mercifully miss Hertfordshire except for a short stretch at the county's eastern fringe, but it should reduce the amount of traffic on both A10 and A11 – the first major road plan we have come across that will actually be a relief to the county rather than a liability. The A11, which will benefit most, is the shortest of the county's roads on which I have based the chapters of this book. Entering Hertfordshire north of Harlow, it passes through Sawbridgeworth and Bishops Stortford and crosses the county boundary again into Essex after a mere seven miles, but I will use it as the axis for discussion of the villages that lie along the eastern border of Hertfordshire as far north as the Pelhams and Meesden. It is a route characterized, even more than the others we have followed, by scattered hamlets with names derived from the bits of common land which formed their focal points – Kettle Green, Kate's Green, Perry Green, Washall Green.

Our first stop is Eastwick, near the River Stort, where Sunday morning anglers on the north bank sit facing the daunting prospect of Harlow across the Essex border. The chief interest of this little village is its church of St Botolph, for although it was rebuilt in the nineteenth century, it has a chancel arch remaining from the thirteenth, which Pevsner calls "astonishingly ambitious", and an effigy of a knight, of similar date, which the same authority calls the best in the county. The church also contains memorials of various members of the Plumer family, whom we shall meet again shortly.

High Wych, a couple of miles away across Fiddler's Brook, also has a nineteenth-century church, but it is singularly unattractive and need not detain us, especially since we are (as you may not have realized) in a hurry to get to Hunsdon. This village, like so many around the borders of Hertfordshire, seems not to belong to the county, its weather-boarded houses near the village pump being distinctively East Anglian. As for the public house which claimed, last time I was there, to be "Britain's Craziest", I cannot judge its entitlement to such distinction, but if there is to be any debate, I am certainly willing to propose a motion that it is the unsightliest. However, it is Hunsdon House, halfway between the village and Eastwick, that is of particular interest to us here.

Henry VIII built a moated palace on the site of an earlier house here, and the raising of his children was shared between this place and Hatfield. At Hunsdon Mary taught her half-sister Elizabeth to play card-games. The King visited the house frequently, and among other visitors to the royal household was Bishop Ridley, whose abortive attempts to convert Mary Tudor to Protestantism were, for him, stepping stones on the way to the stake at Oxford, though the Duke of Norfolk had told the stubborn princess that, if she had been *his* daughter, he would have banged her head against the wall until it was as soft as a baked apple. After Mary's death, the mansion became the property of the Carey family for a long period, during which a brass plate to a park keeper, James Gray, was placed in the adjacent church, showing Death hunting him as he hunted deer.

By the beginning of the nineteenth century Hunsdon had come into the possession of the Calvert family, and Nicholson Calvert, a brewer who became Tory M.P. for Hertford, rebuilt the place on a much smaller scale, though his wife still found it a "dreadfully expensive" job. She, beautiful, intelligent and Irish, was Frances Pery, the daughter of Viscount Glentworth, a former Speaker of the House of Commons. Hunsdon seemed to have a tradition of card-playing, for the Hon. Mrs Calvert played too, but was tempted to give up when she lost £7 once, unlike her friend the Duchess of Devonshire, who died leaving enormous gambling debts. Mrs Calvert had other interests. She started a village school, inoculated the villagers against smallpox, and learned from the village cobbler how to make shoes. But it is for her diary that we are specially indebted to her. Frances Calvert knew everybody and put them in her diary – the Cecils, Caroline Lamb, the Duchesses of Devonshire and Rutland. Above all, she gave us a graphic description of an early nineteenth-century polling day; when in the running with her husband for two seats in Parliament were the Hon. Edward Cowper, son of the third Earl, and the Tory Lord Cranbourne, the Marquess of Salisbury's son. Calvert himself was a Liberal who held his seat for thirty-five years, and his wife was rather put out when Lord Cranbourne had the impertinence to oppose him. It is worth quoting her account of polling day, 8 October 1812, in full:

> On Tuesday morning, a little after seven, James Knox and I set off for the election in my barouche. We took four horses from Waltham Cross to make a figure, and adorned with blue favours made a very fine one. A crowd was gathered round the hustings. Everyone was most kindly interested for us. The state of the Poll was brought me by some friend or other, every quarter of an hour. Mr C. after the start was always at the head of the poll, which was not closed till quite dark, when the returning officer declared the state as follows: Calvert, 365, Cowper, 316, Cranbourne, 256.
>
> The two former were therefore declared duly elected. Mr C. came forward and made a good speech – well heard and much applauded; but as to Mr Cowper they made such a noise with mingled groans and hisses that not one word could be heard, nor could I hear a word of Lord Cranbourne's either. By this time it was so dark that it was not thought safe to chair them, as Lord C's mob was very riotous, so it was put off till the next morning. During the whole of the day, Lord C's mob were terribly noisy. He had a band of music, and I was half deafened by the uproar. Lady Salisbury and Lady Cecil arrived in a landau a little before three, but I believe were not enchanted by the state of things, and went away long before the close of the poll. I must own I was not sorry to have their high blood pulled down a little. Lady Cowper and all the Cowper family came to see me through the mob, which I could have excused as I wished to avoid all

appearance of a coalition. I never saw Mr C. in such good spirits and we all rejoiced that the little Lord was beat. We dined with Mr Dallinger our agent. I found some of our friends the electors there, and, though dreadfully tired, I never felt more pleased. When we reached Hunsdon the bells were ringing merrily for our success.

A short distance up the road from Hunsdon is Widford, and here again it is a house outside the village, rather than the village itself, which demands our notice, for a mile to the west is Blakesware, built on the site of a house well known to readers of Charles Lamb, where his grandmother, Mary Field, was housekeeper to the aforementioned Plumer family who owned it. Lamb visited her often there, and knew the old house inside out. It was there where Charles learned to spell 'plumb-pudding' with a 'b', so that it looked "fatter and more suetty". Undoubtedly the house was the source of much of that irresistible sense of humour which allowed him much later to write to the poet John Clare:

> Since I saw you, I have been in France and have eaten frogs. The nicest little rabbity things you ever tasted. Do look about for them. Make Mrs Clare pick off the hind quarters, boil them plain, with parsley and butter. The fore-quarters are not so good. She may let them hop off by themselves.

In the year after Lamb's visit to Paris, however, the mansion in which his grandmother had served for more than fifty years was pulled down by Walter Plumer, and Lamb was very shocked to see its total demolition:

> Where had stood the great gates? What bounded the courtyard? Whereabout did the out-houses commence? a few bricks only lay as representatives of that which was so stately and so spacious. Death does not shrink up his human victim at this rate. The burnt ashes of a man weigh more in their proportion.

Lamb sat in the Bell Inn to contemplate this destruction, in the village where he had fallen in love for the first time, and where the churchyard contains the bones of his grandmother, who died in 1792, "bent down with age and pain and rankling malady", and those of many others he had known.

The heavier soil in this area of Hertfordshire lent itself readily to the increase in dairy farming which took place around the turn of the century, partly as a direct result of London's growing need for milk supplies, partly because of the enterprise of Scottish migrants who were expert dairy-farmers and who took advantage of cheap land and the new railways to introduce a type of agriculture which, in a time of declining rural population, required less labour for its management. During the last quarter of the nineteenth century there was a big increase in the area of land in Hertfordshire converted from arable to pasture, and the number of dairy cattle in the county almost doubled. A large proportion of the change occurred in this eastern part of the county. But the railway line that helped to bring it here has now been taken away again.

Sawbridgeworth lies beside the A11 to the east of Widford. Built round its old market square, with a number of weatherboarded houses of East Anglian type, its church of St Mary the Great contains a good many memorials to the families who made the town not only prosperous but also well populated, as is evidenced by the multitudinous progeny represented on their monuments. In spite of much dreary modern building, and the arrival by the kerbsides of the thin yellow line that divides unspoilt rural England from the onset of urban fever, Sawbridgeworth is an attractive small town, from the square of which Sheering Mill Lane winds down to the river.

Among the longest-surviving of local families were the Jocelyns, who lived at Hyde Hall close to the River Stort on the very edge of the county. One of their members of the Plantagenet period was twice Lord Mayor of London, but a later Jocelyn who has no monument in the church was Sir John, who died in 1741 and insisted on being buried *with his horse* outside consecrated ground, and so gave the superstitious cause for rumour that his ghost rode his steed down the avenue leading to the house.

The former prosperity of Sawbridgeworth was based on the malting and milling industries, and a group of maltings, much altered, can still be seen on the banks of the Stort, which forms the county boundary for a few miles until it flows into the Lea near Ware. This part of the river had been made navigable as far as Bishops Stortford by Sir George Duckett and his engineer Thomas Yeoman, and had been of some value to the two malting towns on this eastern side of Hertfordshire, but not as much as might have been hoped, and eventually the Stort Navigation was sold to the Lea Conservancy Board for the princely sum of five shillings.

Between the two towns is the village of Thorley, noted for its moated fifteenth-century manor house, Thorley Hall, and for the tradition that the manor was owned by Richard Whittington, the famous cat-fancier and Lord Mayor of London on three occasions in the late fourteenth and early fifteenth centuries. The origins of the legend of Dick and his moggy, which have been the subject of pantomime for centuries, are obscure, but when Whittington had become rich and lent money to the kings of England, one of his acts was to rebuild Newgate Prison, and this serves as a reminder of another owner of Thorley manor, the notorious hanging judge, Lord Chief Justice Ellenborough.

When a bill was proposed to the House of Lords in 1810 to abolish the death penalty for shoplifting, Lord Ellenborough made his famous statement that, if the bill were made law, no man would be able to "trust himself for an hour out of doors without the most alarming apprehensions that, on his return, every vestige of his property will be swept off by the hardened robber". It is said that Ellenborough's own death was hastened by the shock of being contradicted by a jury. Presiding over the trial for blasphemy of William Hone, who was a friend of Charles Lamb, Ellenborough directed the jury to find him guilty, but they refused to do so and acquitted him, thus striking two blows for liberty with one verdict.

Bishops Stortford stands on a tongue, which is Hertfordshire's eastern extremity, poking rudely into Essex. It lies about the crossing of the river by the Roman road later called Stane Street, and gets the first part of its name from the fact that it was owned by the Bishops of London for 800 years. It became prosperous through its malting and tanning industries, and at one stage had what amounted to a monopoly on the supply of charred malt to the London porter brewers, being so well placed to receive its barley supply from the Essex and Cambridgeshire farmers as well as from those of Hertfordshire. This pre-eminence passed to Ware in the nineteenth century, but Bishops Stortford still has its old maltings by the river. The railway had greater significance for this town than the canal, and its population has increased considerably since the mid-nineteenth century.

The uneven ground on which the town stands gives an interesting appearance to its streets, which have some nice old timbered inns and houses, but they have to be sought out now among the modern development that has spoilt the town visually. The parish church has an odd-looking tower, extended in brick above the original flint in 1812, when a spire was also added. Inns that were once famous have been demolished. The Grapes became notorious in 1903, when its licensee was hanged for murdering three wives; but the old Reindeer had already been famous for centuries then. It was a brothel in Samuel Pepys' day, kept by one Elizabeth Aynesworth, and Pepys says that "all the good fellow of the county come hither". It stood at the corner of High Street and Market Square.

Waytemore Castle was the stronghold of the bishops. Nothing remains of it now, but it possessed a prison which was of greater ill-repute than the Reindeer, particularly in Bishop Bonner's day, and may well have had something to do with the receptiveness of Bishops Stortford folk to Nonconformity; the Quakers, among others, having made many converts here. The town had at least five Nonconformist ministers who had been ejected from their livings elsewhere - mainly in Essex.

The most famous Quaker in the town was Thomas Dimsdale, not born here but a resident who is buried in the old Quaker burial ground. He was a doctor who practised at Hertford for many years, and sat for the county town in Parliament. An early practitioner of inoculation against smallpox, he was invited by Catherine the Great to go to Russia to inoculate her and her son the Archduke Paul. Completing the mission successfully, Dimsdale was made a Baron of All the Russias in addition to receiving a handsome fee and an annual allowance for life, and his descendants held the title until the Communist Revolution.

Bishops Stortford gave the world a son of its own even more famous, however. Better known than Pope Adrian IV, Sir Arthur Evans and even Graham Greene, he was the man who has had a far greater influence on the world than any other native of Hertfordshire. He was born here in 1853, the son of the vicar of St Michael's Church, and within fifty years he was dead, but he had made a vast fortune in less time that it took Rockefeller, and he had started a train of events that affects the nations of the world to this day.

There are still those, I dare say, who would call Cecil Rhodes a great man, but I am not among them. His life was an act of compensation for a sickly body and perhaps for sexual inadequacy, and, like Hitler's, it developed into megalomania. He was sent to Africa at an early age when he was found to be tubercular, and he had a large holding in the Kimberley diamond mines by the time he was twenty-one, forming the De Beers Mining Company a few years later. When he was thirty-seven, and a monopolist in industry, he became also a dictator in politics, as Prime Minister of the Cape, conquering the Matabele shortly afterwards and founding Rhodesia.

It was there, in the Matoppo Hills, that he was buried in 1902, forty-nine years after his birth at the vicarage in Bishops Stortford, with a brass plate on his tomb saying simply: "Here lie the remains of Cecil John Rhodes." No need of dates or explanations: he knew the world would remember him. The Boer War was still being fought when he died of heart failure, his body corrupted by his illnesses and his mind and actions by his power. His father had wanted him to become a parson like himself. How different the world might be now if the vicar's will had prevailed. But Cecil Rhodes moved so far from his modest Christian upbringing that he believed that

Britain should rule the world. It is at least arguable – I put it no stronger – that if there had been no Rhodes, there would have been no Boer War, no First World War, no Hitler. And his bloody legacy to Africa will colour our newspapers for many years yet.

Let us hasten westward to Much and Little Hadham, attractive villages of which Much Hadham, in particular, is one of the most stylish in the county, due to the architectural distinction of its main street. Little Hadham was the home of the Capel family whose sons became Earls of Essex. Little Hadham Hall was built in the sixteenth century, but it has been much altered and partly destroyed by fire. Arthur, Lord Capel, who lived there, was executed by Cromwell for his loyalty to Charles I, unlike his son who died in the Tower after plotting to kill Charles II.

Much Hadham was the country home of the Bishops of London for nearly a thousand years, and it is an uncommonly charming and opulent-looking village befitting the wealth of the bishops who owned it. Its timbered cottages mix happily with the fine mansions of the seventeenth- and eighteenth-century gentlemen who lived there, and parts of its pavements in front of them are still cobbled. The H-shaped Bishop's Palace, lying close to the large and well-preserved village church, is perhaps not quite the building we would expect. It is a long gabled house encased in brick, and it has suffered a good deal of alteration, having served as a girls' school at one time, and as a lunatic asylum at another. There was born Edmund of Hadham, who became Earl of Richmond and died in Carmarthen Castle, a prisoner of the Yorkists, leaving a pregnant widow who gave birth to the future Henry VII.

The fine seventeenth-century rectory, and the stone carvings of strange creatures inside the church, seem a trifle at odds with the spanking new (or at any rate, newly painted) clock face on the tower wall, but that will not remain so brightly blue for long, and it at least indicates the care taken to preserve the good looks of this very interesting village.

Most famous among Much Hadham's rectors was Alexander Nowell, who lived to be ninety-four in days when that was much more remarkable than it seems now. Whether his longevity had anything to do with his discovery of bottled beer is not recorded, but it was Izaak Walton who gave him the credit for this 'invention'. It seems the rector was an enthusiastic fisherman, who once left his beer, in a leather bottle, by the river. When he recovered it, some days later, it had a fine head on it and was all the better for being left, and the word soon spread, increasing the prosperity of Hertfordshire brewers and the satisfaction of Hertfordshire drinkers. Nowell became Dean of St Paul's afterwards, where his sermons were liable to be interrupted by Queen Elizabeth telling him to change the subject, particularly if the subject happened to be the danger to the State of the Queen's failure to marry.

A nineteenth-century curate of Albury, just up the road from Little Hadham, was a rather less conscientious churchman. He was inclined to bribe the congregation to return home to save himself the trouble of delivering a sermon at all! Such is the variety of men who enter the Church, as in other professions. A Nonconformist minister of Little Hadham named Daniel Skingle was imprisoned in 1700 at the instigation of that same zealous vicar of Hitchin, Francis Bragge, who was later to be involved as a principal witness in the prosecution of the 'witch' Jane Wenham.

The routes we have followed in theory through Hertfordshire cover many hundreds of miles, but the distance from Aldbury with a 'd' near Tring to Albury without one near Bishops Stortford, is no more than 30 miles. Albury is a widely scattered village with its church some way from its main community. In a corner of the church's north aisle, together with the parish chest, is the tomb of a late fourteenth-century knight and his wife, thought to be Sir Walter and Lady Margaret de la Lee. Their mutilated effigies are covered with the graffiti of centuries of inconsiderate visitors who have scratched their initials on the lady's gentle breast and on her husband's armour, but nothing can detract from the poignant simplicity of this couple who have lain side by side in the church for nearly 600 years. One of the church bells, lost in 1800, was said to be buried in the mud at the bottom of Albury's village pond, reputedly as deep as the church tower is high.

Scattered about the north-eastern boundary of Hertfordshire above Albury, on the high ground at the petering out of the eastern Chilterns, are Great and Little Hormead and the villages called Pelham – Furneaux, Stocking and Brent. All three Pelhams were owned by the Bishops of London. Furneaux is the largest of them. It is called 'Furnix' locally, in consequence of the Englishman's stubborn refusal to pronounce foreign names properly. This country is remote from the major roads, and many more Ends and Greens are dotted about, with quaint or graphic names – Patient End, East End, Puttock's End, Crab Green. Elderly folk who have spent their whole lives in and around the villages of their birth have a different scale of values from those of us who have grown up to take flying and travelling on motorways very much for granted. An old labourer answering my enquiry for a village about two miles away said: "Yer've a fair ol' way ter goo yit, me ol' flower."

The area is characterized by a good deal of thatch, small churches, of which Little Hormead's is typical, standing on the highest bits of ground in the villages, and the preservation of a remarkable number of village pumps, those infallible signs of the original centre of a settlement's foundation – the water supply which is the basic necessity for all human life.

The manor house at Furneaux Pelham was the home of the Calvert family whose path we crossed at Hunsdon. It was said at one time, no doubt with poetic exaggeration, that they could walk down the east side of Hertfordshire on their own land. The church of St Mary contains memorials to them, among which are very fine stained-glass windows by William Morris and Edward Burne-Jones.

A small family brewery in this peaceful country village was one of the last survivors of a considerable number that existed at one time. It was noted for a brew called 'Old Crony' which enjoyed a high reputation among the local populace, but not with the local vicar, who was appalled by the drinking that traditionally took place in such villages after the harvest had been safely gathered in. An urbanite clergyman at heart, no doubt, Rev. Wigram attempted to put a stop to the customary 'drinking day' public holiday, which he called "the great abuse in the parish". He did not, of course, succeed. He ought to have followed the injunction on his own church clock – "Time flies – mind your business."

The winding road from this village across to Braughing is, I think, one of the most enjoyable walks in the county on a sunny day. It really is not possible to say that the influence of London is evident in this delightful countryside, where we come next to Stocking Pelham, which, with its tiny church next to a farm, and its thatched and weatherboarded Cock Inn, is on the very edge of the county, the tiniest of the three Pelhams. Its curious first name appears to come from words signifying land cleared of tree stumps, which also occur in field names in the area.

Brent Pelham is notable chiefly for its legend of a local dragon-slayer, Piers Shonks, whose supposed tomb is in the wall of the church, somewhat archly proclaiming that nothing remains of St George except the legend, but Shonks's bones are here, as if to prove his feat. The name of the village is a corruption of Burnt Pelham, from the fact that a fire in the twelfth century destroyed the whole village, and one wonders if the fable of Piers Shonks, who was a landowner, has been passed down in folklore interpreting the fire as the dragon he slew. Although the village is small, it had sufficient need of its own stocks and whipping post in crueller days, and they can still be seen on the grass beside an attractive thatched cottage.

Finally, we come to Meesden, remotely situated on the Essex border. It cannot, by any stretch of the imagination, be called a pretty place, but its main centre of population is half a mile away from the site of its old church, indicating a shift of settlement, and it may well be that Meesden had a close shave with total desertion, for even before the Black Death its fields were left unploughed for lack of manpower, and its Lammas Day passed by uncelebrated. (This was the 1 August thanksgiving for the first products of the wheat-harvest, the name being derived from 'loaf-mass'. It was observed in many Hertfordshire villages, some of which, including Meesden, had common land called Lammas.)

The survival of this village is an apt reminder of the Hertfordshire dilemma as we end our tour through the county, for Meesden could be called a symbol of the good fortune of the major part of Hertfordshire in resisting the despoliation wrought by advancing civilization. The village lies in the vicinity of Anstey and Nuthampstead, and it might have been another casualty of the third London airport development.

We have been noticing many of the physical changes in the Hertfordshire landscape throughout the course of this book, and before we leave the county we might usefully - with remote rural communities like Meesden in mind - consider other changes, some threatened, some already achieved, which the people of Hertfordshire will probably suffer in silence.

IX

EPILOGUE

From my window I can see arable land which has been cultivated with ploughs pushed by men and hauled successively by oxen, horses and tractors, since Saxon farmers first cleared the forest over a thousand years ago. Although I am not a native of Hertfordshire ("Who *is*?" one might ask), and have been cured of superstition by upbringing in a materialistic Midland environment, I recognize the myths which have grown out of this soil as a part of English life now threatened by the mindless spread of the concrete forest – cutting out light and air once more from land won, by centuries of toil and good husbandry, from primeval sterility.

It is what has happened between times – between the uncontrolled jungle of nature and the corrupt jungle of civilization – that has formed the spiritual character of the Hertfordshire whose physical appearance and local events we have been exploring, and we cannot understand the county unless we look a little more deeply at the people whom the land has made, and who have given their lives to the land in return. If this long and slow process of natural evolution is what Karl Marx meant when he presumptuously referred to "the idiocy of rural life", I believe the countryman is entitled to smile indulgently at the prophet of equality and point to the mental hospitals scattered about the 'civilized' part of Hertfordshire. To this condition, apparently, all mankind is destined to be raised up.

The Anglo-Saxon farmers who began to turn this land into a fertile source of food imposed themselves on a sparse native population of small dark people who were nominally Christian, but who cherished a great deal of pagan folklore derived not from the Romans, who would have had little influence on the small communities scattered about the countryside, but from the Celtic settlers who preceded them. Rural communities have much longer memories than urban ones. The different pace of life encourages rumination, and oral tradition dies hard. There are beliefs which were current in this county in the time of Boudicca that still have an observable, if tenuous, hold on the imaginations of the country folk. Christianity may have coloured such beliefs; even distorted or disguised them. But it has not destroyed them. They are too deeply implanted in the collective unconscious of the people. Christianity did not replace the beliefs it found here – it merely overlaid them with a set of new ones which obscured the older and deeper layer beneath.

Charles Lamb, in a short essay on puns, quotes with obvious pleasure one that, if we did not know it was invented by Swift, we should surely attribute to some pun-loving native of Hertfordshire: "An Oxford scholar, meeting a porter who was carrying a hare through the streets, accosts him with this extraordinary question: 'Prithee, friend, is that thy own hare, or a wig?' "

That farmland animal, rarely seen by townsfolk, has figured in the mythology of the ancient Greeks and various other peoples, including the Saxons, as a symbol of fertility and magic. There is a tradition that Boudicca carried a hare into battle against the Romans, releasing it among them in the belief that it would strike fear into her enemies. Christianity was forced to embrace the many Celtic superstitions about it, because they refused to fade away. The *Boke of Saynt Alban's* calls the hare "the marvellest beest that is in any londe", and there is a graffito of a hare in St Albans Abbey. The animal was closely associated with witchcraft, and Mother Haggy of St Albans was one of those who was supposed to be able to turn herself into a hare. Another was Sally Deards, the witch of Rabley Heath, near Welwyn, who was shot dead by a gamekeeper, it is said, during her ill-chosen metamorphosis.

Of the many ancient country superstitions surrounding the animal, the most recent survivals are those associating the hare with good or bad luck, and a hare's foot as a sort of charm against illness. One belief that may still persist in Hertfordshire is that if you see a hare run through a village street, it is a sure sign that a fire will break out. Put it down to coincidence, if you like, that the poet William Cowper, some years after his confinement at Doctor Cotton's Home for Madmen at St Albans, kept hares – so often associated with madness – as very unusual pets.

Other beliefs about animals among the gullible rustics were that swallowing a young frog was a cure for asthma, (a precursor of shock therapy, perhaps), and that on Christmas Eve, oxen in their stalls would kneel down, facing the east.

As well as the many ghost stories in the county, Hertfordshire folklore is replete with tales of witchcraft, as we have seen. Sir Francis Bacon may have written, 400 years ago, that "witches themselves are imaginative and believe oft-times they do what they do not; and people are credulous in that point, and ready to impute accidents and natural operations to witchcraft". But the beliefs of the uneducated country folk were too deeply etched in their souls to be altered by mere logic. They thought Bacon himself was a wizard of sorts, with a secret underground passage from Gorhambury to St Albans Abbey, and to this day one occasionally hears of supposed witchcraft rearing its wizened old head here and there in Hertfordshire. No wonder old Jane Wenham had to be given sanctuary by Lord Cowper after Judge Powell had released her. She would have been lynched by the credulous mob. As I write, early in 1977, a 39-year-old Stevenage woman has been sentenced to life imprisonment at St Albans Crown Court for the murder of a lonely old spinster at Hitchin. The defendant described herself as a witch, and was said to frighten local children by threatening to turn them into toads.

Is it any wonder that ancient fertility rituals and beliefs should have been carried into that most elemental part of the Hertfordshire cycle of life, the harvest? They were transferred into Christian practice in such forms as Plough Sunday, when ploughs were taken into church to be blessed, and in 'beating the parish bounds', when the lord of the manor, the parson and a procession of villagers walked round the circumference of the parish calling for God's blessing on the growing crops. It was thought unlucky to get married between the hay and the harvest, so July weddings were rare in Hertfordshire, but it was counted lucky to see a hay-wagon, when one was supposed to make a wish as it passed by. We noticed in Chapter V that No Man's Land, near Wheathampstead, was supposed to be disputed territory between neighbouring bishoprics. But possibly the name has earlier origins than that. There was an ancient belief that one piece of land in every parish was taboo to the farmers, who left it uncultivated as a sacrifice to the Devil, who would not then wither the crops in the rest of the parish – hence 'no man's land'. The last sheaf of corn to be cut was called the 'Corn Baby' and it was ceremoniously carried on top of the last load, which was called the 'Hockey Load'. The custom was for the villagers to throw water over this load as it travelled from field to barn, in a ritual fertilization of the spirit of the corn, and this ancient procedure survived the Church's attempt to convert it into Christian practice as the harvest festival.

The harvesters worked under one of their number whom they had elected as 'Lord of the Harvest'. He was a sort of rustic shop-steward, who negotiated the labourers' terms with the farmer and set the pace at which they would work. William Cobbett described a journey into Hertfordshire in the summer of 1822, when he saw squads of labourers

> leaving the fields cleared behind them. The mowers, with their scythes on their shoulders, were in front, going on towards the standing crops, while the haymakers were already coming on behind towards the grass already cut or cutting. The weather is fair and warm, so that the public houses on the road are pouring out their beer pretty fast . . .
>
> The custom is in this part of Hertfordshire to leave a border round the ploughed part of the fields to bear grass to make hay from, so that, the grass now being made into hay, every corn-field has a closely mowed grass walk ten feet wide all round it, between the corn and the hedge. This is most beautiful.

"What that man ever invented, under the name of

pleasure-grounds," Cobbett went on, "can equal these fields in Hertfordshire?"

A good man could reap four acres of barley a day with a scythe, but there were hard times, and women and children had to learn straw-plaiting or some other craft to save the family from starvation. Lace-making was another local speciality. The farmers had to give a tenth of their crops to the parson as the church levy known as 'tithes'. One of the teachings of John Ball, the Lollard martyr, was that people should not pay tithes to the curate unless they were better off than the curate was, but of course this was an outrageous affront to the capitalist Church, and Thomas Walsingham, the St Albans monk, condemned Ball for teaching "the perverse doctrines of the perfidious John Wyclif", and as we have seen, he paid dearly for such revolutionary ideas.

How could Hertfordshire Thickheads (who were called Hertfordshire Hayabouts when they were recruited into the militia, because they did not know left from right and wore a grass on one leg and a straw on the other, so they could be ordered to turn 'hay-about' or 'straw-about') – how could these people be expected to absorb new ideas, think for themselves and turn away from the authority of the lord and the parson whom they and their forefathers had obeyed for centuries? They had tilled the soil under the successive rules of the Romans, the Saxons and the Norman lords, and then under the local squire, who represented power, wealth and authority. Industry was not yet on the horizon, the great movement of rural population into the towns had not begun, and education was a privilege reserved for the sons of the better-off.

Can we be surprised that the rustic peasants were slow to learn the lessons of the Reformation? There had been ample demonstration at St Albans, the spiritual centre of the county, of what happened to rebels who tried to change the established order of things. The mass of the people remained docile, kept out of trouble, and allowed the county to become a stronghold of Conservatism. That old lady who believed that Mary Ansell must be guilty of murder "because they were hanging her" was a true daughter of Hertfordshire, and the remark of a worker quoted in one book for the sake of his dialect is equally revealing of a general state of mind: "Wunt 'ear a word agin my maaster; dunt keer oo tolt yer."

The influence of industry and commuterism on the religion of Hertfordshire would be a most rewarding field of study for some student of sociology. In this largely rural population, the slow progress of religious dissent before the Industrial Revolution is almost wholly attributable to the authority of the squire and the parson over people whose lives moved unhurriedly through an annual cycle, the pattern of which seemed preordained by God or Nature. Apart from the influence of Lollardry from the Chiltern dens of Nonconformity in the west, there was only a marginal growth of Puritanism through the centuries. True, there were Hertfordshire men who joined Cromwell's army, and Hertfordshire families who sailed to America, like Thomas Olney, a shoemaker and his wife and two children, and John Tuttell, a mercer and his wife and their sixteen-year-old servant. There were unwilling emigrants too, especially among the Quakers, nine of whom were sentenced at Hertford to be "transported beyond the seas to the island of Barbadoes, there to remain for ever". These nine were lucky. After spending two months aboard ship waiting for suitable weather to sail, they were freed when the ship's master gave up the attempt.

Congregationalists infiltrated the county from the east, via East Anglia and the emigrant Brownists in Holland, while Baptists spread southwards from Bedfordshire under the powerful influence of Bunyan and his disciples. A strong centre of the Particular Baptists was Kensworth, which, together with Studham, was in Hertfordshire at that time, and a link developed between the Baptist communities there and at St Albans, the latter having thirty-five members in 1750. There are many records of persecution, both of ministers and their congregations. George Kendall, a minister at Hemel Hempstead, was imprisoned for refusing to baptize infants, and at Hertford one Samuel Goodman, brought before the ecclesiastical court for teaching school without a licence, pleaded that he merely instructed "Blew Coate boyes belonging to Christ's Hospital . . . in the art of writing and arithmetic". The Exton family of Walkern was fined for failing to pay the rate towards the repair of the parish church, and for not attending divine service on Sundays and holy days. The Quakers, increasingly numerous in the county, suffered most of all, but then, their behaviour was unorthodox as well as their beliefs, and as they, more than other sects, tended to attract the poor and illiterate (hence their relative success in Hertfordshire!), they were regarded as a greater threat to the *status quo*. Their emphasis on private conscience did not impress Bunyan, who said: "Conscience is a poor dunghill creature in comparison of the Spirit." But the Quakers retorted that Bunyan's teaching was "foule lyes and slanders".

None of these influences, however, was of dramatic proportions in the county. The country people at large continued to attend their local parish churches, untouched by the tide of religious ferment that was sweeping through the larger towns. When the lord of the manor was a Protestant, of course, as were the Bacons at Gorhambury and the Dutch Wittewronge family at Rothamsted, there was likely to be a growing Nonconformist influence. Besides the Particular Baptists in St Albans, there were a number of Methodists in Harpenden after James II's Toleration Act. In the rural areas, even those who did profess Nonconformism often attended services in the parish church. The spiritual freedom which the spread of Nonconformism brought was a matter of relative indifference to the illiterate rural worker, but the rise of capitalism which came with it was definitely against his interests. Economic exploitation by the landlord was worse than spiritual exploitation by the Church. And enclosure of the open fields was the country cousin of business capitalism in the towns, both being related by marriage, as it were, to the rise of Nonconformism.

Enclosure was in the interests of urban economy, but not of equality and co-operation in rural communities. Though necessary for improvement of the nation's food production, it brought increased poverty to agricultural workers. No longer owning their own strips of land, their wages kept low by rising population, they were at the same time deprived of sidelines like straw-plaiting by the growth of factory industry. Sir Francis Bacon had seen long before that enclosure would breed "a decay of people, and by consequence a decay of towns, churches, tithes and the like". But it was, ironically, the urban population which soon began to protest against over-enclosure, which was, although slow in coming to Hertfordshire, destroying the common land which the townsfolk wanted preserved for their recreation. The fiasco of Lord Brownlow's attempted enclosure of Berkhamsted Common was a typical case of the townsman preserving what the farmworker would have relinquished. Such are life's paradoxes.

Since the rise of industry, with the accompanying growth of the New Towns and the rapid increase in 'overspill' population, more dramatic religious changes have taken place, like the expansion in the number of Methodists in the county in recent years, producing a situation in which the proportion of Nonconformists increased while at the same time church membership was in rapid decline. There has been an increase, also, in essentially urban Christian fringe groups such as the Seventh Day Adventists, and also in the population of Jews in the county, all attributable to the drift northwards of Londoners and the creation of new resident populations. And hand in hand with these urban communities has come the inevitable growth of industry, a more breathless pace of life, the rivalry of materialistic standards, and the stresses of overpopulated areas.

Hertfordshire has no university to give it a radical student voice, nor a significant coloured immigrant population to create racial tensions, so changes in attitude, though progressing through the county steadily, are perhaps less violent than one would expect from the rapid and startling alterations to the landscape. But modern technology affects farm as well as townscape. Large fenced fields begin to replace the small fields bounded by hedges and trees, in order to make more economical use of agricultural machinery, and those

Hertfordshire fields that Cobbett found so beautiful will gradually disappear. The distinctions that William Cowper saw when he said that "God made the country, and man made the town" are no longer quite so clear.

Just after the turn of the century, Rider Haggard wrote:

> In this twentieth century England we seem to have grown away from the land; we have flocked into cities; we have set our hearts on trade, and look to its profits for our luxury. But the land is still the true mother of our race, which, were it not for that same land, would soon dwindle into littleness.

Well, if we *are* dwindling into littleness, it is small comfort that the rural tradition of Hertfordshire may survive that of some other counties.

George Orwell's appalling vision of the very near future seems unduly pessimistic now, but it is fair warning against complacency, which is the luxury Hertfordshire can least afford, but the one in which it is, by its very nature, most apt to indulge. The threat of urban development now comes from the north as well as the south, as Luton looks to expand its living space, like London. The healthy air of the old Hertfordshire is to be squeezed out of it like the juice of a lemon as the county is slowly throttled by industrial expansion and its spiritual character burned up by the flowing lava of civilization's erupting volcano, levelling everything in its path and producing that dreadful standardization and uniformity of work, behaviour, noise and pollution which is – as I remarked at the beginning of this book – the lip of hell upon which Hertfordshire is uneasily perched. It is all very well for government departments and local authorities to point cheerfully to 'Green Belt' legislation, but the question is: What shade of green? Some of the county's so-called Green Belt has already been blancoed with military-style barbarism into a muddy khaki.

The cultural and recreational needs of Hertfordshire's new intelligentsia are somewhat delicately poised at present between the home-made and the metropolitan. Rural organizations like rambling clubs and (at the other end of the social scale) weekend shooting parties still cater for those who prefer the old country pursuits, but for the new urban society bingo rushes into the vacuum of redundant cinemas and the deep-freeze takes over the role of status symbol now that 'everyone' has a car and colour television.

The arts move into Hertfordshire with pussy-footed cautiousness – bookshops are of infrequent occurrence and indifferent standard, and art galleries non-existent. Amateur dramatic societies, like the Company of Ten and the Abbots Langley Gilbert and Sullivan Society, provide sufficient theatre for local needs at present, when real enthusiasts can so easily get to the West End. One of the few original contributions the county has made to the arts, so far, is the biennial St Albans International Organ Festival. In all other respects, Hertfordshire follows rather than leads.

More obvious changes are taking place in the county's old image of a Tory paradise. Industrial Watford and Nonconformist Hitchin became Labour constituencies years ago, and in the late 1974 election the New Town constituencies threw out long-standing Conservative members for candidates who were not only Socialists but, more significantly, were very much younger than the rejected members. In the case of Welwyn and Hatfield, Helene Middleweek (now Mrs Hayman), a 25 year-old former President of the Cambridge Union, won the seat from Lord Balniel, who had been the Conservative member for Hertford for nearly twenty years. The 'posh' residential areas will remain Conservative, of course, but a county in which the Tories hold only half the seats can no longer be called "the Mecca and El Dorado of Conservatism".

So, in these times when nothing stands still, Hertfordshire is being dragged along in spite of itself, though not always for the better. 'Progress' in its more threatening form rises up and looms over us in the shape of buildings like the Kodak block in Hemel Hempstead, the Smith Kline & French building at Welwyn Garden City, and the hideous swimming baths at Hatfield. Some future historian, no doubt, will be writing of this area of England in much the same way that one might write of Lancashire or South Yorkshire, mentioning such agricultural land as remains only as an incidental relief from the towns, industry, noise, traffic, pollution and mental stress which will finally have driven out all traces of the county's 2,000 years of rural tradition. By that time, however, Hertfordshire will no longer exist as such. The Maud Commission on local government reorganization, in the late 'sixties, proposed that Hertfordshire should be abolished altogether and divided between two new local authorities. The next chapter in the county's story may well be 'The Way to Oblivion'.

Perhaps we should allow the Cecils the last word. Lord David Cecil recounts that his uncle William, the Bishop of Exeter, had thought of a plan for heating a room by placing radiators under armchairs, to which Lord David objected that this would not be comfortable as the chairs could not be moved. The Bishop's reply might be taken as a motto – an epitaph, even – for modern Hertfordshire. "My dear boy," he said, "when one is putting in a heating system, comfort must go to the wall."

SOURCES

1. BOOKS ABOUT HERTFORDSHIRE

William Andrews (ed.), *Bygone Hertfordshire* (Andrews & Co., 1898)
B. J. Bailey, *Ashridge Observed* (Inglenook Press, 1975)
Mary Carbery & Edwin Grey, *Hertfordshire Heritage* (Green & Co., 1948)
Sir Henry Chauncy, *The Historical Antiquities of Hertfordshire* (London, 1700)
Robert Clutterbuck, *The History and Antiquities of the County of Hertford*, 3 vols (London, 1815-27)
Olive Cook, *A Study of Anstey* (Nuthampstead Preservation Assn., n.d.)
John Edwin Cussans, *History of Hertfordshire*, 3 vols (Chatto & Windus, 1870-81)
K. Rutherford Davis, *The Deserted Medieval Villages of Hertfordshire* (Phillimore & Co., 1973)
W. B. Gerish, *Hertfordshire Folk Lore* (S. R. Publishers edition, 1970)
W. B. Gerish (compiler), unpublished *Dictionary of Hertfordshire Biography*
J. E. B. Gover, Allen Mawer & F. M. Stenton, *The Place Names of Hertfordshire* (Cambridge University Press, 1938)
Reginald A. Hine *The History of Hitchin*, 2 vols (Eric T. Moore, 1972)
W. Branch Johnson, *Hertfordshire* (Batsford, 1970)
Doris Jones-Baker, *Old Hertfordshire Calendar* (Phillimore, 1974)
Arthur Mee, *The King's England: Hertfordshire* (Hodder & Stoughton, 1965)
Nikolaus Pevsner, *The Buildings of England: Hertfordshire* (Penguin Books, 1953)
C. A. Manning Press, *Hertfordshire Leaders* (McCorquodale & Co., 1894)
Rudolph Robert, *Historic Hertfordshire* (Letchworth, 1968)
Nathaniel Salmon, *The History of Hertfordshire* (London, 1728)

W. R. Saunders, *History of Watford* (C. H. Peacock, 1931)

Sir William Beach Thomas, *Hertfordshire* (The County Books) (Robert Hale, 1950)

Herbert W. Tompkins, *Hertfordshire* (Methuen & Co., 1903)

Elsie Toms, *The Story of St. Albans* (Abbey Mill Press, 1962)

William Urwick, *Nonconformity in Herts* (Hazell, Watson & Viney, 1884)

Anthony Wigens, *A View into Hertfordshire* (Terence Dalton, 1970)

Herts Highway Committee, *Review of Policies and Programmes* (Herts C.C., 1973)

Victoria County History of Hertfordshire, 4 vols, 1902–14

Files of *Hertfordshire Countryside*, *Herts Advertiser* and other local journals

2. OTHER WORKS

Horace Bleackley, *The Hangmen of England* (Chapman & Hall, 1929)

Julius Caesar, *War Commentaries* (Everyman's Library edition, 1953)

Lord David Cecil, *The Cecils of Hatfield House* (Constable, 1973)

William Cobbett, *Rural Rides* (Everyman's Library edition, 1973)

G. R. Crosher, *Along the Chiltern Ways* (Cassell, 1973)

H. C. Darby (ed.), *A New Historical Geography of England after 1600* (Cambridge University Press, 1976)

Daniel Defoe, *A Tour through the Whole Island of Great Britain* (Penguin edition, 1971)

Bonamy Dobrée, *Sarah Churchill, Duchess of Marlborough* (Gerald Howe, 1927)

George Ewart Evans and David Thomson, *The Leaping Hare* (Faber & Faber, 1972)

Peter Ferriday, *Lord Grimthorpe* (John Murray, 1957)

John D. Gay, *The Geography of Religion in England* (Duckworth, 1971)

Graham Greene, *A Sort of Life* (Bodley Head, 1971)

Charles Hadfield, *The Canals of the East Midlands* (David & Charles, 1966)

Reginald L. Hine, *Charles Lamb and His Hertfordshire* (Dent, 1949)

W. G. Hoskins, *The Making of the English Landscape* (Hodder & Stoughton, 1955)

Ada C. Kopeć, *The Distribution of the Blood Groups in the United Kingdom* (Oxford University Press, 1970)

K. B. McFarlane, *Wycliffe and the Beginnings of English Nonconformity* (Penguin edition, 1972)

Iona & Peter Opie, *The Lore and Language of Schoolchildren* (Oxford University Press, 1959)

George Perry, *The Great British Picture Show* (Hart-Davis, MacGibbon, 1974)

Peter Quennell, *Byron – The Years of Fame* (Collins, 1935)

Bertrand Russell, *Autobiography*, Vol. II (Allen & Unwin, 1968)

R. L. Sherlock, *British Regional Geology: London and Thames Valley* (H.M.S.O., 1960)

Tacitus, *The Annals of Imperial Rome* (Penguin edition, 1975)

Eric R. Watson (ed.), *Trial of Thurtell and Hunt* (Notable British Trials) (William Hodge & Co., 1920)

Norman W. Webster, *The Great North Road* (Adams & Dart, 1974)

R. E. M. & T. V. Wheeler, *Verulamium – A Belgic and two Roman Cities* (Society of Antiquaries, 1936)

Emlyn Williams, *Emlyn* (Bodley Head, 1973)

Philip Ziegler, *The Black Death* (Collins, 1969)

Lee Valley Regional Park Authority, *Report on the Development of the Regional Park with Plan of Proposals* (Enfield, 1969)

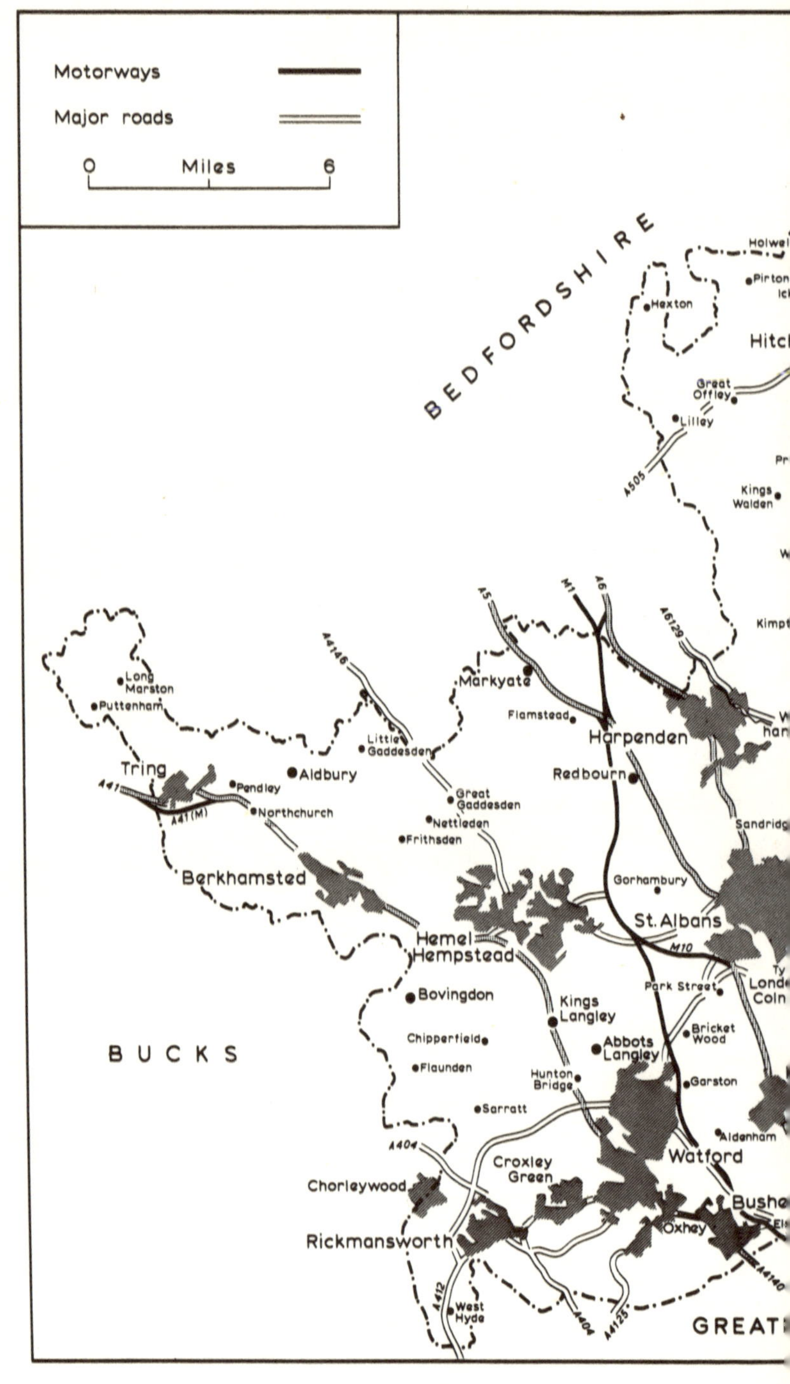

Motorways
Major roads
0
Miles
6
BEDFORDSHIRE
Hexton
Pirton
Great Offley
Lilley
A505
Kings Walden
Kimpt
A5
M1
A6
A6129
A4146
Long Marston
Puttenham
Markyate
Flamstead
Harpenden
Little Gaddesden
Redbourn
Tring
Aldbury
Pendley
A41
A41(M)
Northchurch
Great Gaddesden
Nettleden
Frithsden
Sandridg
Berkhamsted
Gorhambury
St. Albans
Hemel Hempstead
M10
Park Street
Bovingdon
Kings Langley
Bricket Wood
Chipperfield
Abbots Langley
BUCKS
Flaunden
Hunton Bridge
Garston
Sarratt
Aldenham
A404
Watford
Croxley Green
Chorleywood
Oxhey
Rickmansworth
A4140
A412
West Hyde
A404
A4125
GREAT

Based with permission on the Ordnance Survey

INDEX

Note: Hertfordshire has a large number of villages whose names are prefixed by 'Little', 'Great', etc., and I have thought it preferable to index them by their common prefixes. Thus, Little Munden is to be found under 'Little' and not under 'Munden'.